THE LITTLE
BLACK BOOK OF

PARIS

*The Essential Guide to the
City of Light*

VESNA NESKOW

ILLUSTRATED BY KERREN BARBAS

PETER PAUPER PRESS, INC.
WHITE PLAINS, NEW YORK

FOR TANYA AND PETE,
WHO FIRST GAVE ME THE
GIFT OF TRAVEL

Illustrations copyright © 2006 Kerren Barbas
Paris Metro Map © 2006 La Régie Automone des Transports
Parisens (RATP). Used with permission.
Neighborhood maps © 2006 David Lindroth Inc.

Designed by Heather Zschock

Copyright © 2006
Peter Pauper Press, Inc.
202 Mamaroneck Avenue
White Plains, NY 10601
All rights reserved
ISBN 1-59359-850-5
Printed in Hong Kong
7 6 5 4 3 2 1

THE LITTLE
BLACK BOOK OF

PARIS

CONTENTS

INTRODUCTION

P aris conjures visions of sophistication, drama, and romance. The clichés abound, yet there's no denying the allure and beauty of the City of Light. Flamboyant and mysterious, Gothic and modern, refined and bawdy—Paris is all these, with room for both grandeur and coziness. It is a city imbued with history, a center of art, culture, and fashion, a cauldron of the intellectual avant-garde. But it is also a city of well-tended gardens, of cafés highly suited to people-watching, a feast of grand architectural splendors and small delights around every corner. And speaking of feasts, the food's not bad, either!

Paris is best seen on foot, walking up and down narrow passages and wide boulevards. With map in hand, it's hard to get lost. But what a treat it is to meander through the streets, taking in unexpected pleasures at nearly every step.

We encourage you to do just that: wander the streets as you visit the sites in this guidebook. There are so many extraordinary places in Paris that we've kept to our favorites, those exemplifying Paris as a center of style and re-invention, both historically and today. By exploring the city you'll discover what you love most.

Paris is divided into numbered sectors called "*arrondissements*," postal codes by which Parisians identify locations. However, we've arranged this guidebook by clusters of neighborhoods, or quarters. (You will find that we have included the *arrondissements* within the specific addresses of sites.) The first seven chapters cover such clusters in central Paris, each with its own map. The eighth chapter highlights places on the city's outskirts and the ninth chapter includes short excursions to spots near Paris. We've also included an overview map of the entire city inside the front cover and a public transportation map in the back.

Once you've explored Paris and been enchanted by its beauty and spirit, you can quote Humphrey Bogart when, in the movie *Casablanca*, he tells Ingrid Bergman, "We'll always have Paris."

GREAT VIEWS

For the best—and it's free!—sightseeing tour, walk along the Seine River. The views are spectacular. Be sure to look down at the walkways bordering the water: you'll see lovers kissing beneath the trees, students poring over books, fishermen patiently holding a line in the water, and the occasional beret-topped *grand-père* calmly feeding the pigeons.

You'll find other great views from atop the Eiffel Tower, the steps and terraces of Sacré-Coeur, the Georges restaurant on the roof of Beaubourg (Centre Georges Pompidou), the roof of the Institute of the Arab World, and, following in the footsteps of Quasimodo, the North Tower of Notre Dame.

For a river view, ride a tourist boat *(bateau-mouche)* along the Seine. **Bateaux-Mouches** depart from the Alma Bridge *(T. 01-42.25.96.10, www.bateaux-mouches.fr).* **Bateaux Parisiens** depart from Port de la Bourdonnais, near the Eiffel Tower *(T. 01-46.99.43.13, www.bateaux parisiens.com).* **Vedettes du Pont-Neuf** *(Square du Vert Galant, Paris 1st, T. 01-46.33.98.38, www.vedettes dupontneuf.com)* are open boats. Or catch the **Batobus** *(T. 08-25.05.01.01, www.batobus.com),* public transportation on the river, at any of its eight stops between the Eiffel Tower and the Jardin des Plantes.

HOW TO USE THIS GUIDE

We have included a map for each neighborhood with color-coded numbers corresponding to the places mentioned in the text. **Red** symbols indicate **Places to See** (landmarks and arts & entertainment). **Blue** symbols indicate **Places to Eat & Drink** (restaurants, cafés, bars, and nightlife). **Orange** symbols indicate **Where to Shop**. **Green** symbols indicate **Where to Stay**. Some restaurants are closed in August, so check before going.

Here are our keys for restaurant and hotel costs:

Restaurants
Cost of an appetizer and main course without drinks

(€)	Up to 25€
(€€)	25€-45€
(€€€)	45€ and up

Hotels

Cost per night
(€)	50€-125€
(€€)	125€-250€
(€€€)	250€ and up

Abbreviations:

M   métro (subway) station

ALL ABOUT MONEY

Money changing

The currency in France is Euros (€). ATMs abound and most places take credit cards. Visa is commonly called "Carte Bleue" and MasterCard is often referred to as "Eurocard." Exchange rates for cash or travelers' checks are best in banks, but some offer the service for their clients only. Avoid changing money in airports, train stations, hotels, restaurants, and shops. You can try these places:

AMERICAN EXPRESS: 11 rue Scribe, 9th (*M: Opéra (exit rue Scribe), T. 01-47.77.79.50*)

CITIBANK: 125 avénue Champs-Elysées, 8th (*M: Charles-de-Gaulle-Etoile, T. 01-53.23.33.60*)

COMPTOIR DE CHANGE OPÉRA: 9 rue Scribe, 9th (*M: Opéra, T. 01-47.42.20.96*)

MULTICHANGE: 7 rue de Castiglione, 1st (and other locations) (*M: Tuileries, T. 01-40.15.61.16, www.multi-change.com*)

Tipping

A 15% service charge is added to all hotel and restaurant bills in France. But sometimes an additional tip is appropriate. A few extra Euro-cents in a bar or café is fine; up to 10% in a restaurant if the waiter was particularly good. In hotels, tip 1€/bag for bellboys, 1€ for room service, 1€/day for housekeeping. For taxi drivers, tip 10%–15% on meter fares. In hair salons, give 10%–15% for any service.

Got cents?

Decimal points and commas are reversed from the U.S. system. So Euros are separated from Euro-cents *(centimes)* by a comma, and hundreds are separated from thousands by a period. On price tags, a € sign often replaces the decimal point (8,50€ = 8€50).

PUBLIC TRANSPORTATION

Getting to and from the Airport

Paris's two major airports are Roissy/Charles de Gaulle (CDG) and Orly. Flights from the U.S. generally go to CDG. Free shuttle buses marked "ADP" (Aéroports de Paris) connect the terminals and go to the Roissy RER (regional rapid-transit train/subway) station. The airport RER costs about 9€ one way.

Taxis into town cost about 65€ during off-hours, more at peak hours. Car and van services require reservations (16€–20€ per person). Aéroport Limousine Service *(T. 01-40.71.84.62)* is a fixed-fare car service. Airport

Connection *(T. 01-44.18.36.02)* is a door-to-door minibus service. Airport Shuttle is another van service *(toll-free: 0-800-699-699)*.

Non-reservation buses include the Air France Bus, about 12€ *(T. 01-41.56.89.00, recording in French and English)*, and RoissyBus, the RATP city bus, about 9€ *(T. 01-48.04.18.24)*.

More information on getting into the city is available at:
www.parisnet.net/info_airplane.html
www.parisnet.net/parishuttle.html
www.paris.org/Accueil/Airport
www.worldairportguide.co.uk/airports/cdg/cdg.asp
www.paris-cdg.com

Métro, RER, SNCF, and Travel Passes

"Le Métro" is the subway. Individual métro/bus tickets cost 1€40 and a book of 10 tickets *(carnet)* costs 10€70. Visitors' passes are also sold at métro stations and online. Métro lines are identified by different numbers and colors. There is a fold-out Paris métro map in the back of this book. The métro runs daily from 5:30 AM to 12:40 AM.

The **RER** is a system of commuter trains that transports people from the outskirts of Paris into the central city. Many of the stations overlap with the métro stations and can be used interchangeably (tickets and passes are valid for both within the city). There are five different lines (A, B, C, D, and E), each with a different color. These are indicated on the map in the back of the book with slightly thicker lines than the métro lines. In some cases, it might be quicker to use an RER train to get from one destination to another because there will be fewer stops in between, than on the métro train. The RER trains run daily from 5:30 AM to 1:00 AM.

There are five **SNCF** *(reservations and information: 08-92.35.35.35, open daily 7:00 AM to 10:00 PM, www.sncf.com)* rail train stations that travel much further out of the city. These can be used for long-distance destinations and excursions. The station names appear in boldface type in the map at the back of the book, and the lines are a light gray color. You would use these for destinations featured in Chapter 9.

Paris Visite is a pass for 1, 2, 3, or 5 consecutive days of unlimited travel on the métro or buses *(www.parisvisite.com/en/index.php)*. Some passes are for Paris only; others include outskirts.

PHONE NUMBER, S'IL VOUS PLAÎT?

When calling Paris direct from the U.S., dial 011-33 then drop the initial 0 in the number. When dialing within France or within Paris, dial the number as it appears (with the initial 0).

SHOPPING

Sales: By law, sales *(soldes)* are held twice a year in France, in January and July. In Paris they last a month. At other times of year, good deals are marked in stores as "*promotions.*"

Tax refunds: If you spend a minimum of 175€ in one store, you can get a tax refund *(détaxe)*. You must show your passport and fill out a form in the store. On leaving at the airport, go to the "*bureau de détaxe*" to get your forms stamped. Do this before going through passport control or baggage check-in: you may have to show your purchases. Back home, return the pink copy in the envelope provided; keep the other for your records. If traveling to other EU countries, get your forms stamped in the airport customs office of the last EU country you leave. It takes about three months to get the refund.

Duty-free shops: Best at airports. The duty-free shops around Opéra and Palais Royal aren't much of a deal.

Chain and discount stores: Fnac is a chain store great for books, CDs, and electronics. Paris's main discount chain stores are Prisunic and Monoprix.

SAY IT IN FRENCH

Although it's best to carry a phrase book, here are a few basic words and phrases to get you started.

Bonjour *(bohn-zhOOR)* Hello; good morning/day
Bon soir *(bohn sWAH)* Good evening
Au revoir *(or-vwAR)* Good-bye
S'il vous plaît *(sill voo plEH)* Please
Je voudrais... *(zhuh voo-DRAY)* I would like …
Merci *(mare-sEE)* Thank you
Oui *(wEE)* Yes
Non *(nOH)* No
Où est... *(oo ay...)* Where is …
le métro *(luh meh-tRO)* subway
un carnet *(un car-nAY)* packet of 10 subway tickets
un billet *(un bee-yAY)* ticket
la rue *(lah rOO)* street
l'hôtel *(low-tEL)* hotel; house/mansion
le magasin *(magazEHN)* store
le grand magasin *(gran magazEHN)* department store
le restaurant *(restorON)* restaurant
Parlez-vous anglais? *(par-lay voo ohng-LAY)*
    Do you speak English?
Où sont les toilettes? *(oo sohn les twalET?)*
    Where is the bathroom?
Ça coûte combien? *(Sah koot kombee-EN?)*
    How much does that cost?
Madame *(mah-dAHM)* Ma'am; Mrs.
Mademoiselle *(mahd-mwa-zEL)* Miss
Monsieur *(muss-YUH)* Sir; Mr.

ETIQUETTE TIP

Whether it's "Bonjour," "Au revoir," "Merci," or "S'il vous plaît," it's rude to address someone without saying "Madame" or "Monsieur" after the address. On entering a shop, always first say, "Bonjour, Madame/Monsieur." If you enter a store with a man and a woman clerk, greet both with, "Bonjour, Madame, Monsieur." Even the surliest Parisian waiter will say hello! Just don't call him "garçon"—it means both "waiter" and "boy" and is considered rude. Better to say, "S'il vous plaît, Monsieur."

BOOKING TICKETS

You can buy theatre and concert tickets at any **Fnac** *(one branch is at 74 ave. des Champs-Elysées, 8th, M: George V, T. 01-53.53.64.64, www.fnac.com)* or **Virgin Megastore** *(52–60 ave. des Champs-Elysées, 8th, M: Franklin D. Roosevelt, T. 01-49.53.50.00)* and also at **Carrousel du Louvre** *(99 rue de Rivoli, M: Concorde, T. 01-44.50.03.10)*. Same-day, half-price tickets (commercial fare) sell at **Kiosque de la Madeleine** *(15 pl. de la Madeleine, 8th, M: Madeleine or Concorde, closed Monday)*. Most theatres are closed on Mondays. Magazines with listings for arts and entertainment are available at newsstands—in French, every Wednesday: *Pariscope*; *L'Officiel des Spectacles*; and *Zurban*; in English: *Paris Free Voice* and *The City* (quarterly).

Paris Museum is a pass for 1, 3, or 5 consecutive days of unlimited visits to museums (permanent collections) and monuments. Kids under 18 enter most museums free; those 18 to 25 years old at reduced rates. See the following Web sites for more information:

www.museums-of-paris.com/museum-pass.php
www.conciergerie.com
www.discoverfrance.net

SEASONAL EVENTS

Winter-Spring:

Salon des Grands Vins, early Feb., wine tastings & workshops *(Carrousel du Louvre, 99 rue de Rivoli, 1st, M: Palais Royal, www.salondesgrandsvins.com)*

Printemps des Poètes, Mar., national poetry festival *(various venues, www.printempsdespoetes.com)*

Paris Film Festival, April *(various venues, T. 01-45.72. 96.40, www.festivaldufilmdeparis.com)*

Summer:

French Tennis Open, May-June *(Stade Roland Garros, 2 ave. Gordon-Bennett, 16th, M: Porte d'Auteuil, T. 01-47.43.48.00, www.frenchopen.org)*

Quinzaine des Réalisateurs, May-June, films from the Cannes Festival *(Forum des Images, Porte St-Eustache, Forum des Halles, 1st, M: Les Halles, T. 01-44.76.62.00, www.forumdesimages.net)*

Paris Jazz Festival, June-July *(Parc Floral de Paris, Bois de Vincennes, 12th, M: Château de Vincennes, T. 08-20. 00.75.75, www.parcfloraldeparis.com)*

INVALIDES
CHAILLOT
CHAMPS-ELYSÉES

Places to See:

1. Pont Alexandre III
2. Hôtel des Invalides
3. Assemblée Nationale
4. Hôtel Matignon
5. Eiffel Tower
6. Rodin Museum
7. Sewers
8. La Pagode
20. Palais de Chaillot
21. Trocadéro Gardens
22. Musée du Vin
23. Musée Guimet
24. Palais de Tokyo
25. Palais Galliéra Fashion Museum
26. Maison de Radio-France
35. Arc de Triomphe
36. Grand Palais
37. Petit Palais
38. Elysée Palace
39. Place de la Concorde
40. Atelier Renault
41. Théâtre des Champs-Elysées
42. L'Atelier des Chefs
43. Musée Jacquemart-André

Places to Eat & Drink:

9. Aux Ducs de Bourgogne
10. Bistrot le P'tit Troquet
11. Jules Verne
12. Café Constant
13. Les Fables de la Fontaine
14. Le Violon d'Ingres
27. L'Astrance
28. La Table du Joël Robuchon
29. Cristal Room
30. Tokyo Eat
44. Boutiques Vignon
45. Atelier Renault Café/Bar
46. Pierre Gagnaire
47. Restaurant Guy Savoy
48. Monte Carlo Restaurant Buffet
49. BE Boulangépicier
50. L'Écluse François-1er
51. Nirvana

Where to Shop:

15. Loulou de la Falaise
16. Maison Poujauran
31. Avenue Victor Hugo
52. Harel
53. Inès de la Fressange
54. D. Porthault

If you are lucky enough to have
lived in Paris as a young man,
then wherever you go for the rest
of your life, it stays with you, for
Paris is a moveable feast.

—Ernest Hemingway

INVALIDES

8 **13** *to Invalides;* **12** *to Assemblée Nationale;*
13 *to Varenne;* **8** *to École Militaire;*
6 *to Bir Hakeim (Tour Eiffel)*

● SNAPSHOT ●

Over its colorful history, Invalides has been refuge to torn and tattered soldiers, a tool of rebellious crowds, and home to Napoleon's tomb. From monuments to government buildings to 18th-century aristocratic town houses, the Invalides area exudes *hauteur* and beauty on a grand scale. It is the Left (southern) Bank's equivalent of Right (northern) Bank grandeur. It's home to the renowned Eiffel Tower, the magnificent Rodin Museum, and other "not-to-be-missed" sites.

PLACES TO SEE
Landmarks:

The Art Nouveau lamps of the ornate, exuberant **Pont Alexandre III (1)** *(off of ave. du Maréchal-Gallieni, 8th)* create an elegant curve bridging the Seine River. The gilded statuary—cherubs, nymphs, and winged horses—of this flamboyant bridge leads directly to the **Hôtel des Invalides (2)** *(Esplanade des Invalides, 7th, 01-44.42.37.72, www.invalides. org)* on the Left Bank. Commissioned by Louis XIV as a hospital for French soldiers, Invalides now houses several military museums, notably the **Musée**

de l'Armée, and **Napoleon's Tomb** (under the gilded baroque dome). East of Invalides, along the Seine, is the **Assemblée Nationale (3)**, or Palais Bourbon *(33 quai d'Orsay, 7th, 01-40.63.00.00, www.assemblee-nat.fr)*, the lower body of the French parliament. The Prime Minister resides at the **Hôtel Matignon (4)** *(57 rue de Varenne, 7th, closed to public)*.

On the other (west) side of Invalides is the **École Militaire** with its vast training ground, the **Champ de Mars** (great for jogging). At the far end of this park, bordering the Seine, is Paris's most renowned sight, the cast-iron **Eiffel Tower (5)** *(Champ de Mars, 7th, 01-44.11.23.23, www.tour-eiffel.fr)*. Observation platforms at all three levels provide spectacular views, next to souvenir shops, cafés, and exhibitions. The stunning night view of Paris from the Eiffel Tower may leave you breathless; and for ten minutes every hour a dazzling 20,000-bulb light show makes the ironwork seem magical.

Arts & Entertainment:

The **Rodin Museum (6)** *(77 rue de Varenne, 7th, 01-44.18.61.10, www.musee-rodin.fr)* is one of the best in Paris, with Auguste Rodin's great sculptures on display both inside and in the garden outside. Don't miss *The Kiss, The Thinker, Balzac, The Gates of Hell,* and *The Burghers of Calais*. For a unique underground museum, pop into the **Sewers (7)** *(Égouts de Paris, opposite 93 quai d'Orsay, off the Alma Bridge, 7th, 01-*

53.68.27.81). If you're in the mood for a non-main-stream film, **La Pagode (8)** *(57 bis, rue de Babylone, 7th, 08-92.89.28.92)* shows international independent films.

PLACES TO EAT & DRINK

Lunch at the cozy *crêperie* **Aux Ducs de Bourgogne (9)** (€) *(30 rue de Bourgogne, 7th, 01-45.51.32.48, lunch only)* or order take-outs. The intimate **Bistrot le P'tit Troquet (10)** (€€) *(28 rue de l'Exposition, 7th, 01-47.05.80.39)* serves traditional French food. The food and the views at **Jules Verne (11)** (€€€) *(Eiffel Tower, Level 2, 7th, 01-45.55.61.44, www.tour-eiffel.fr)* are fabulous, but the less expensive Eiffel Tower cafés have the same vista. Chef Christian Constant boasts three restaurants in the area: **Café Constant (12)** (€) *(139 rue St-Dominique, 7th, 01-47.53.73.34)*, **Les Fables de la Fontaine (13)** (€€) *(131 rue St-Dominique, 7th, 01-44.18.37.55)* for seafood, and the exquisite **Le Violon d'Ingres (14)** (€€€) *(135 rue St-Dominique, 7th, 01-45.55.15.05, www.levi olondingres.com).*

WHERE TO SHOP

The boutique of designer Loulou de la Falaise (15) *(7 rue de Bourgogne, 7th, 01-45.51.42.32, www.loulou-de-la-falaise. com)* is awash in vibrantly colored, imaginative clothes and accessories. At Maison Poujauran (16) *(18-20 rue Jean-Nicot, 7th, 01-47.05.80. 88)*, a tiny old-fashioned *boulangerie*, you'll find wonderful *baguettes* and bis-cuits *(sablés)*; it's the official bread

supplier to the Elysée Palace, the presidential residence—credentials well-earned.

WHERE TO STAY

Practical, minimalist rooms make **Grand Hôtel Lévêque (17)** (€) *(29 rue Cler, 7th, 01-47.05.49.15, www.hotel-leveque.com)* a low-budget favorite. For elegance and luxury in the diplomatic neighborhood around parliament, **Bourgogne & Montana (18)** (€€€) *(3 rue de Bourgogne, 7th, 01-45.51.20.22, toll-free from US 800-44-UTELL, www.bourgogne-montana.com)* exudes tradition for a classy clientele. Quiet and hospitable, **Hôtel de Londres Eiffel (19)** (€€) *(1 rue Augereau, 7th, 01-45.51.63.02, www.londres-eiffel.com)* is tastefully outfitted.

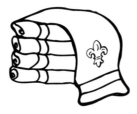

CHAILLOT

6 **9** *to Trocadéro;* **9** *to Iéna or Alma-Marceau;*
2 *to Victor Hugo;* **1** **2** **6** *to Ch. de Gaulle-Étoile*

• SNAPSHOT •

"Opulent" and "staid" best describe the exclusive Chaillot quarter. The village of Chaillot was annexed into Paris and underwent surgery during the modernizations of Baron Hausmann, under Napoleon III, to become a neighborhood of grandeur for the *haute bourgeoisie*. It is arguably one of the best places in Paris to catch phenomenal views of the city and its treasures.

PLACES TO SEE
Landmarks:

Facing the Eiffel Tower, across the Seine past the Iéna Bridge, is the monumental **Palais de Chaillot (20)** *(17 pl. du Trocadéro, 16th)*. Its two curved neoclassical wings, harsh and cumbersome, provide great photo ops from the central terrace: a magnificent view of the river and the Eiffel Tower. The **Trocadéro Gardens (21)** *(16th)* sweep down from the terrace, around a long, central pool of fountains bordered by statues.

Arts & Entertainment:

The **Palais de Chaillot (20)** *(see also above)* houses several museums: for architecture, the **Cité de l'Architecture et du Patrimoine** *(01-.44.05.39.10)*; for

25

anthropology and archaeology, the **Musée de l'Homme** *(01-44.05.72.72, www.mnhn.fr)*; and for French maritime history, the **Musée de la Marine** *(01-53.65.69.69, www.musee-marine.fr)*. For the history of winemaking (and tastings), visit the **Musée du Vin (22)** *(Rue des Eaux, 16th, 01-45.25.63.26, www.museeduvinparis.com)*. The **Théâtre National de Chaillot** *(01-53.65.31.00)* in the **Palais Chaillot (20)** *(see also page 25)* stages classics and some musicals. Nearby is the **Musée Guimet (23)** *(6 pl. d'Iéna, 16th, 01-56.52.53.00, www.museeguimet.fr)*, one of the world's major museums of Asian art. The neo-classical **Palais de Tokyo (24)** *(13 ave. du Président-Wilson, 16th, 01-47.23.38.86, www.palaisdetokyo.com)* is notable for its stunningly redesigned interior. It houses the **Museum of Modern Art** in the east wing and the **Site de Création Contemporaine** in the west wing. Versatile, dynamic, and imaginative, the space morphs for each exhibit's needs. The café terrace affords a great view of the Seine. Paris fashion shows are by invitation only, but the **Palais Galliéra Fashion Museum (25)** *(Musée de la Mode et du Costume, Palais Galliéra, 10 ave. Pierre 1er de Serbie, 16th, 01-56.52.86.20, www.paris-france.org/musees)* holds two or three French fashion exhibits per year. Free concerts at **Maison de Radio-France (26)** *(116 ave. du Président-Kennedy, 16th, 01-53.92.01.23, www.radiofrance.fr)* feature classical music and well-known popular musicians.

PLACES TO EAT & DRINK
Where to Eat:
Celebrity chef Pascal Barbot's culinary creations at **L'Astrance (27)** (€€€) *(4 rue Beethoven, 16th, 01-40.50. 84.40)* are superb; it's tiny, so book months in advance. Equally *magnifique* is **La Table du Joël Robuchon (28)** (€€€) *(16 ave. Bugeaud, 16th, 01-56.28.16.16)*. For a trip into surreal fantasy, the Philippe Starck-designed **Cristal Room (29)** (€€€) *(11 pl. des États-Unis, 16th, 01-40.22.11.10, www.baccarat.fr)* is very hot. The décor reflects the eccentricity of the mansion's former owner, Marie-Laure de Noailles, friend of Cocteau, Dalí, Man Ray, and Buñuel. Or opt for a sandwich at one of the many elegant cafés on the Place du Trocadéro. The post-modern **Tokyo Eat (30)** (€€€) *(Palais de Tokyo, 13 ave. du Président-Wilson, 16th, 01-47.20.00.29)*, the restaurant at the **Palais de Tokyo (24)** *(see also page 26)*, is as much an artistic and aesthetically pleasing experience as it is a culinary one.

Bars & Nightlife:
This staid neighborhood isn't known for nightlife. But there's a cultural night scene at the **Palais de Tokyo (24)** *(see also page 26)*, whose fabulous exhibits of international art are open until midnight.

WHERE TO SHOP

A host of fashion designers display their work in boutiques along Avenue Victor Hugo (31), among them **Apostrophe** (No. 5), **Givenchy** (No. 66), and **Stéphane Kélian** (No. 20). The style strength of this particular avenue can best be described in two words: conservative and classic.

WHERE TO STAY

This area is not very exciting for tourists; it is well suited for business travelers. For casual French chic, **Au Palais de Chaillot Hôtel (32)** (€) *(35 ave. Raymond Poincaré, 16th, 01-53.70.09.09, www.chaillotel.com)* offers bang for the buck. The rooms at **Hôtel du Rond-Point de Longchamp (33)** (€€) *(86 rue de Longchamp, at pl. de Mexico, 16th, 01-45.05.13.63, www.rd-pt-longchamp.fr)* vary in décor from Louis XIV to efficiently modern.

CHAMPS-ELYSÉES

1 **2** **6** *to Ch. de Gaulle-Étoile;*
1 *to George V or FDR;* **9** *to Alma Marceau;*
1 **13** *to Champs-Élysées-Clemenceau;*
1 **8** **12** *to Concorde*

● SNAPSHOT ●

The Champs-Élysées district and the Place Charles-de-Gaulle (or Place de l'Étoile) epitomize the spirit of the *grands boulevards*. Twelve wide avenues radiate from the rotary of l'Étoile ("star"), cutting a grandiose swath through majestic *fin-de-siècle* residences. Despite the infiltration of commercialism on Champs-Élysées Avenue, the quarter is among the city's most aristocratic—and among the most popular for tourists who wish to take in perhaps the most famous avenue of the city. But the area is not just a tourist spot—it hosts numerous events and spectacular displays of national pride on days such as Bastille Day and New Year's Eve.

PLACES TO SEE
Landmarks:

In the center of Étoile, an island in a sea of moving vehicles, stands the **Arc de Triomphe (35)** *(Pl. Charles-de-Gaulle/Étoile, 8th, 01-55.37.73.77).* Commissioned by Napoleon to commemorate his army's victories, the enormous

arch is adorned with sculptures depicting battle scenes. Beneath it lies the tomb of the Unknown Soldier. Once the focus of fashionable society, the **Avenue des Champs-Elysées** has lost much of its aristocratic cachet but remains Paris's most famous street. The **Grand Palais (36)** *(Porte A, ave. Général-Eisenhower, 8th, 01-44.13.17.30)*, an imposing exhibition hall with a magnificent glass-roofed central atrium, mixes classical stonework with Art Nouveau ironwork, topped with galloping bronze horses. Architecturally similar, the **Petit Palais (37)** *(Ave. Winston Churchill, 8th, 01-44.51.19.31)* exhibits the city's collection of French and Renaissance art. Its dome mirrors the Invalides cupola directly across the river. North of the Champs-Elysées, the beautiful **Elysée Palace (38)** *(55 rue du Faubourg-St-Honoré, 8th, closed to the public)* with its English gardens, is the official residence of the president of the Republic. At the eastern end of the Champs-Elysées, the **Place de la Concorde (39)** *(8th)*, with its beautiful fountain, is a focal point for major landmarks: the **Arc de Triomphe (35)** (west) *(see also page 29)*, the **Madeleine church** (north), the **National Assembly** (south), and the **Tuileries Gardens** and **Louvre**

(east). At the center of the square is a 75-foot-tall **obelisk**, covered in hieroglyphics, from the temple of Luxor, an 1831 gift to France from Egypt. Louis XVI, Marie-Antoinette, Danton, and Robespierre all lost their heads here when the guillotine reigned.

Arts & Entertainment:

Besides the museums mentioned earlier, it's fun to visit the **Atelier Renault (40)** *(53 ave. des Champs-Elysées, 8th, 01-49.53.70.70, www.atelier-renault.com)* where cars aren't only on the showroom floor, they're on the walls too. The top classical music and opera concert venue is the **Théâtre des Champs-Elysées (41)** *(15 ave. Montaigne, 8th, 01-49.52.50.50, www.theatrechampselysees.fr)*. Or take a cooking class at **L'Atelier des Chefs (42)** *(10 rue de Penthièvre, 8th, 01-53.30.05.82, www.latelierdeschefs. com)* in a glass-roofed loft. **Musée Jacquemart-André (43)** *(158 bd. Haussmann, 8th, 01-45. 62.11.59, www.musee-jacquemart-andre.com)*, once the home of banker Édouard André and portraitist Nélie Jacquemart, is an extravagant jewel containing an extraordinary collection of paintings, tapestries, and furniture.

PLACES TO EAT & DRINK
Where to Eat:

Find gourmet take-out at **Boutiques Vignon (44)** (€) *(14 rue Marbeuf, 8th, 01-47.20.24.26)*. Drugstore Publicis (59) (€€) *(133 ave. des Champs-Elysées, 8th, 01-47.20.39.25)*, good for a quick bite, is a stylish general store with restaurants and a pharmacy. The **Atelier Renault Café/Bar (45)** (€) *(53 ave. des Champs-Elysées, 8th, 01-49.53.70.70, www.atelier-renault.com) (see also page 31)* is a perfect people-watching place. An avant-garde, extravagant food experience for gourmets, **Pierre Gagnaire (46)** (€€€€) *(Hôtel Balzac, 6 rue Balzac, 8th, 01-58.36.12.50, www.pierre-gagnaire.com)* dazzles as it delights. **Restaurant Guy Savoy (47)** (€€€) *(18 rue Troyon, 17th, 01-43.80.40.61, www.guysavoy.com)* combines country inn hospitality with sensuous gastronomy. The cafeteria-style self-service at **Monte Carlo Restaurant Buffet (48)** (€) *(9 ave. de Wagram, 17th, 01-43.80.02.20/21)* is a great bargain for the area. It has many dishes to choose from and even comes with wine. Celebrity chef Alain Ducasse does gourmet sandwiches in his deli/bread shop **BE Boulangépicier (49)** (€) *(73 bd. de Courcelles, 17th, 01-46.22.20.20, www.boulangepicier.com)*.

Bars & Nightlife:

With a wide selection of wines to sample, along with seasonal French dishes, **L'Écluse François-1er (50)** *(64 rue François 1er, 8th, 01-47.20.77.09, www.lecluse baravin.com)* is a trendy wine bar. There's a line to get into the hip club **Nirvana (51)** *(3 ave. Matignon, 8th,*

01-53.89.18.91), but it's friendly and the dance floor rocks (the restaurant is expensive).

WHERE TO SHOP

In the triangle of **avenues George V**, **Champs-Elysées**, and **Montaigne** is an embarrassment of riches, overflowing with designer fashion houses. In Avenue Montaigne you'll find handmade shoes at Harel (52) *(8 ave. Montaigne, 8th, 01-47.23.83.03)*, women's wear at Inès de la Fressange (53) *(14 ave. Montaigne, 8th, 01-47.23.08.94)* (she's the official face of France, traditionally called "Marianne"), and French linens at D. Porthault (54) *(18 ave. Montaigne, 8th, 01-47.20.75.25)*. For specialty foodstuffs Fouquet (55) *(22 rue François 1er, 8th, 01-47.23.30.36)* is a dream. Trente-Huit François Premier (56) *(38 rue François 1er, 8th, 01-47.20.73.13)* offers last year's women's and men's designer clothes up to 70% off.

Men's shirts and neckties are the focus at Alain Figaret (57) *(14 bis rue Marbeuf, 8th, 01-47.23.35.49)*; men's hats at Hermès-Motsch (58) *(42 ave. George V, 8th, 01-47.23.79.22)*. There's everything from toys to books to shampoo at Drugstore Publicis (59) *(133 ave. des Champs-Elysées, 8th, 0147.20.39.25)*. The chain store Monoprix (60) *(branch at 52 ave. des Champs-Elysées, 8th, 01-53.77.65.65)* has a variety of good inexpensive items. Next door the Virgin Megastore (61) *(52-60 ave. des Champs-Elysées, 8th, 01-40.74.06.48)* sells CDs, books, and electronics.

Expensive art and antiques galleries line **Avenue Matignon**, as well as a stamp and postcard collectors' market. Artcurial (62) *(9 ave. Matignon, 8th, 01-42.99.16.16)* boasts one of the largest collections of art books in Paris. The **rue du Faubourg St-Honoré** (and its continuation rue St-Honoré) is Paris's most famous street for shopping. *Prêt-à-porter* designer shops abound along with places such as the Anne Sémonin (63) *(108 rue du Faubourg St-Honoré, 8th, 01-42.66.24.22)* day spa and Anna Lowe (65) *(104 rue du Faubourg St-Honoré, 8th, 01-42.66.11.32)*, which offers savings of about 40% on off-the-runway women's designer clothes. Down the street, legendary Roger Vivier (64) *(29 rue du Faubourg-St-Honoré, 8th, 01-53.43.00.00)* shoes are like foot sculpture from the inventor of stiletto heels.

MADELEINE/OPÉRA TUILERIES/LOUVRE/ PALAIS ROYAL

Places to See:

1. Madeleine
2. Opéra Garnier
4. Musée Gustave Moreau
27. Tuileries Gardens
28. Arc de Triomphe du Carrousel
29. Louvre Museum
30. Louvre Pyramid
31. Place Vendôme
32. Palais Royal
33. Galerie Vivienne
34. Galerie Colbert
35. Place des Victoires
36. Jeu de Paume
37. Orangerie
38. Museum of Decorative Arts
39. Comédie Française
40. National Library-Richelieu Branch
41. Legrand Filles et Fils

Places to Eat & Drink:

3. Café de la Paix
5. Fauchon
6. Hédiard
7. Lucas Carton
8. Farnesina
9. Ladurée
10. Cojean
11. Chez Jean
12. La Patata
13. Harry's New York Bar
42. L'Ardoise
43. Ferdi
44. Le Soufflé
45. Lescure
46. Lunchtime
47. L'Écume St-Honoré
48. Le Pain Quotidien
49. Androuët Sur le Pouce
50. Le Carré des Feuillants
51. Angelina
52. Café Marly
53. Le Grand Véfour
54. L'Épi d'Or
55. Le Petit Flore
56. A Priori Thé
57. Chez Georges
58. Café Moderne
59. Aux Lyonnais
60. Bar Hemingway
61. Le Café des Initiés
62. Le Fumoir
63. Le Pulp

Where to Shop:

Where to Stay:

1 **8** **12** to Concorde; **8** **12** **14** to Madeleine;
3 **7** **8** to Opéra; **7** **9** to Chaussée d'Antin

• SNAPSHOT •

In the 19th century Baron Haussmann transformed Paris from a medieval fortress village into a modern city. With extraordinary vision he created wide, open boulevards that gave the city its aura of splendor and assured its place as one of the most beautiful cities of the world. Besides increasing ventilation and integrating the newly extended water and sewer systems, the avenues had the advantage of making it harder for rebellious citizens to erect barricades—a lesson learned from the revolutions which took place between 1789 and 1848. Nowhere is his extraordinary urban planning as visible as in the areas around Madeleine and the Opéra. The opulent use of space, in boulevards as well as buildings, has made it a prestigious location for the headquarters of major banks, while its bustling streets attract tourists, fashionistas, and people-watchers.

PLACES TO SEE
Landmarks:

North of the **Place de la Concorde** at the other end of Rue Royale is the neoclassical church known as **Madeleine (1)** *(Pl. de la Madeleine, 8th, 01-44.51.69.00)*. With its 52 Corinthian columns, it looks like a Greek temple. It faces what could be its mirror-image, the

National Assembly, straight across Concorde and over the river. **Place de la Madeleine** is known for luxury food shops, but it was also home to luminaries: No. 9, for example, was Marcel Proust's childhood house. Follow the majestic **Boulevard des Capucines** and you'll arrive at the **Opéra Garnier (2)** *(Pl. de l'Opéra, 9th, 01-40.01. 22.63)*. Tons of gilt and marble went into building the Paris Opéra. Its mix of styles, ranging from Classical to Baroque, features gold busts, winged angels, rearing horses, and ornate columns. Named after its architect, Charles Garnier, it is emblematic of Second Empire grandeur and excess. Garnier also built the sumptuous **Café de la Paix (3)** *(see also page 41)* on the corner of the Place de l'Opéra and Boulevard des Capucines.

Arts & Entertainment:

The ballet company of the **Opéra Garnier (2)** *(Pl. de l'Opéra, 9th, 08-92.89.90.90, www.opera-de-paris.fr)*

performs classical and contemporary pieces. The Opéra also hosts modern dance companies from around the world. The wonderful **Musée Gustave Moreau (4)** *(14 rue de la Rochefoucauld, 9th, 01-48.74.38.50, www.musee-moreau.fr)* is devoted to this Symbolist painter's art, life, and obsessions.

PLACES TO EAT & DRINK
Where to Eat:

Place de la Madeleine is a cornucopia of restaurants and luxury groceries. **Fauchon (5)** (€€) *(26 pl. de la Madeleine, 8th, 01-70.39.74.14, www.fauchon.com)* is famous for its fabulous delicacies, as is **Hédiard (6)** (€€) *(21 pl. de la Madeleine, 8th, 01-43.12.88.99, www.hediard.fr)*; eat there or take it home. **Lucas Carton (7)** (€€€) *(9 pl. de la Madeleine, 8th, 01-42.65.22.90, www.lucascarton.com)*, in its art nouveau décor, serves divine dishes; the prix-fixe lunch will burn a smaller hole in your pocket. Isabelle Adjani and Inès de la Fressange swear by the fantastic Italian fare at **Farnesina (8)** (€€-€€€) *(9 rue Boissy d'Anglas, 8th, 08-99.65.06.70)*. One of the most classic tearooms in Paris, **Ladurée (9)** (€-€€) *(16 rue Royale, 8th, 01-42.60.21.79)* began as a bakery and sweet shop in 1862. Healthy soups, salads, and sandwiches at **Cojean (10)** (€) *(4-6 rue de Sèze, 9th, 01-40.06.08.80)* feature the freshest produce.

If you're at the Opéra, the **Café de la Paix (3)** (€€€€) *(Grand Hôtel Inter-Continental, 12 bd. des Capucines, 9th, 01-40.07.30.20, www.paris.intercontinental.com)* is an experience, if not for a meal, then at least a *café express*. The saying goes that if you sit there long enough, you'll see all the world go by. **Chez Jean (11)** (€€) *(8 rue St-Lazare, 9th, 01-48.78.62.73)*, with the fresh seasonal creations of its capable chef, is a bargain for nouvelle cuisine. For a cheap eat, **La Patata (12)** (€) *(25 bd. des Italiens, 2nd, 01-42.68.16.66)* offers salads and baked potatoes with a variety of toppings.

Bars & Nightlife:

Café de la Paix (3) *(see also page 41)*, open until 1 AM, is great for a relaxed people-watching evening. Ever classic, **Harry's New York Bar (13)** *(5 rue Daunou, 2nd, 01-42.61.71.14, www.harrys-bar.fr)* is still popular with American ex-pats in Paris.

WHERE TO SHOP

Place de la Madeleine is known for luxury foodstuffs: **Fauchon (5)** and **Hédiard (6)** *(see also page 41)* are practically unbeatable. On the opposite side of the square, Maille (14) *(6 pl. de la Madeleine, 8th, 01-40.15.06.00)*, the famous mustard maker, sells divine mustards, vinegars, and olive oil. The specialty shop Jadis et Gourmande (15) *(27 rue Boissy d'Anglas, 8th, 01-42.65.23.23)* is known for the *tresse*, a chocolate with nuts and candied orange peel. Or, to satisfy the craving for the perfect, small piece of oh-so-slightly bitter chocolate, head for La Maison du Chocolat (16) *(8 bd. de la Madeleine, 9th, 01-47.42.86.52, www.lamaisonduchoco lat.com)*. Clothing at Loft Design by (17) *(12 rue du Faubourg-St-Honoré, 8th, 01-42.65.59.65)* is fashionably black or gray. Treat yourself to some pampering at the beauty salon Institut Carita (18) *(11 rue du Faubourg-St-Honoré, 8th, 01-44.94.11.11)*. Eyeglasses have been the specialty of Lafont et Fils (19) *(11 rue Vignon, 8th, 01-47.42.25.93)* for three generations—conservative or eccentric, they make a fashion statement.

The **Place de l'Opéra** is encircled by specialty boutiques, like Lancel (20) *(8 pl. de l'Opera, 9th, 01-47.42.37. 29)* for leather goods and **Clerc** jewelers. Behind the Opéra on **Boulevard Haussmann** are two of Paris's most renowned department stores: Galeries Lafayette (21) *(40 bd. Haussmann, 9th, 01-42.82.34.56)* and Au Printemps (22) *(64 bd. Haussmann, 9th, 01-42.82.50.00)*, which carry designer ready-to-wear, among other things. Several streets north, L'Atelier du Chocolat de Bayonne (23) *(109 rue St-Lazare, 9th, 01-40.16.09.13)* is famous for its chocolate bouquets. Adorn yourself with some jewelry from Cartier (25) *(13 rue de la Paix, 2nd, 01-42.18.53.70, www.cartier.com)*

WHERE TO STAY

A feng shui expert helped design the Zen-inspired **Golden Opéra de Noailles (24)** (€€) *(9 rue de la Michodière, 2nd, 01-47.42.92.90, US toll-free 800-344-1212, www.hoteldenoailles.com)*. Luxury in a modern setting makes **Park Hyatt Paris-Vendôme (26)** (€€€) *(5 rue de la Paix, 2nd, 01-58.71.12.34, www.paris. vendome.hyatt.com)* the destination for elegant but trendy travelers with deep pockets; the glass conservatory-dining room, with its potted orchids and displays of works by contemporary artists such as Ed Paschke and Llyn Foulkes, is especially pleasing.

TUILERIES/LOUVRE/ PALAIS ROYAL

① **⑧** **⑫** *to Concorde;* **①** *to Tuileries, Palais Royal (Musée du Louvre), or Louvre/Rivoli;* **❸** *to Bourse*

• SNAPSHOT •

The Louvre, the geographic center of Paris, was built as a fortress against the English in 1190. Around 1360 it was transformed into a royal residence, undergoing alterations by successive rulers over the centuries. In 1793 after the French Revolution it was turned into a museum with the royal collection on public display. It remains one of the major museums in the world, with a vast collection of art and antiquities. Stretching between the Louvre and Concorde, the Tuileries Gardens are an extension of the Louvre, with pavilions on either side housing other museums. Together with the opulent Place Vendôme and elegant Palais Royal to the north, this quarter affords a glimpse into the extravagant life of the French rulers and the power and riches of the *ancien régime*.

PLACES TO SEE
Landmarks:

Terraces, alleys, slopes, stairways, and stone pools were carefully planned for the royal **Tuileries Gardens (27)** *(Rue de Rivoli/Quai François Mitterrand, 1st)* situated along the Seine on the eastern border of Concorde. Statues by 19th and 20th-century artists complete the architectural whole with magnificent vistas in every direction. The **Arc de Triomphe du Carrousel (28)**—built to celebrate Napoleon's 1805 victories—stands between the Tuileries and the Louvre. Stand beneath the arch for a fantastic view of Paris, stretching in a straight line from the Louvre through the Tuileries, past Concorde, along the Champs-Elysées, through the Arc de Triomphe, across to the Grand Arch at La Défense, just beyond Paris—an axis covering half the city. In modern counterpoint to the old architectural splendor of the **Louvre Museum (29)** *(Rue de Rivoli, 1st, 01-40.20.51.51, www.louvre.fr)*, architect I.M. Pei's **Louvre Pyramid (30)**, built in 1989 in the courtyard of the Louvre, is at the museum's main entrance. The surrounding reflecting pools create

a dizzying mirror image of the glass and steel structure while small pyramids echo the larg-

er one's effect. The riverfront views are spectacular. Bordering the Tuileries and the Louvre to the north, **Rue de Rivoli**, with its long row of arches, is home to expensive hotels, boutiques, and bookshops.

From Rue de Rivoli, take Rue de Castiglione and you'll arrive at one of Paris's most majestic squares, **Place Vendôme (31)** *(connecting to the Opéra via Rue de la Paix)*. Built by Versailles architect Mansart, the octagonal square is an elegant example of harmonious, graceful 17th-century architecture. Many of the mansions were homes of bankers; one of them, No. 15, is now the **Hôtel Ritz (90)** *(see also page 53)*, where Coco Chanel lived, not far from her *salon de couture*. No. 12 was the house in which Chopin died in 1849. Today, under the arches encircling the square at ground level, **Place Vendôme (31)** is home to the haute jewelers of the world.

Just north of the Louvre is **Palais Royal (32)** *(Pl. du Palais-Royal, 1st)*—which has been through many phases—once Cardinal Richelieu's palace, then the childhood home of Louis XIV, and later the scene of elaborate and lavish gatherings as well as gambling and indulgent, rowdy celebrations. Today its arched court-yard bustles with boutiques and restaurants. Not to be missed are the stunning early 19th-century shopping arcades *(passages* or *galeries)*, with their high vaulted roofs of glass and iron. From the far (north) end of Palais Royal, take Rue Vivienne then turn right onto Rue des Petits Champs. To the left you'll find **Galerie Vivienne (33)** and **Galerie Colbert (34)**—wander into any *galerie*, but be sure to check out these two. Rue des Petits Champs turns into La Feuillade before reaching the elegant fashion mecca, **Place des Victoires (35)** *(Rue la Feuillade, 1st/2nd)*, built around a statue of Louis XIV.

Arts & Entertainment:

Museums abound: the **Louvre (29)** *(see also page 45)* for arts and antiquities, the **Jeu de Paume (36)** *(Jardin des Tuileries, pl. de la Concorde, 8th, 01-47.03.12.50)* for contemporary art, the **Orangerie (37)** *(Pl. de la Concorde, 1st, 01-42.97.48.16)* for great Impressionist works, and the **Museum of Decorative Arts (38)** *(Palais de Louvre, 107 rue de Rivoli, 1st, 01-44.55.57.50, www.ucad.fr)* for art and design and its Art Nouveau and Art Deco collections. Near the Palais Royal entrance, France's finest classical theater is staged at the **Comédie Française (39)** *(2 rue de Richelieu, 1st, 08-25.10.16.80, www.comedie-francaise.fr)*. The **National Library-Richelieu Branch (40)** *(58 rue de Richelieu, 2nd, 01-53.79.53.79, www.bnf.fr)*, north of Palais Royal, became an exhibition space once its books were moved to the Mitterand branch. For a change of pace, **Legrand Filles et Fils (41)** *(1 rue de la Banque, 2nd, 01-42.60.07.12, www.caves-legrand.com)* offers wine courses focusing on a region or producer.

PLACES TO EAT & DRINK

Where to Eat:

The area bordered by Tuileries, Concorde, Place Vendôme, and Palais Royal is replete with cozy restaurants. Though Place Vendôme is one of the priciest spots in town, the nearby **L'Ardoise (42)** (€€) *(28 rue du Mont-Thabor, 1st, 01-42.96.28.18)* is reasonably priced for good New Bistro fare. A few doors down, fashionistas feast on great burgers at lunch and tapas for dinner at **Ferdi (43)** (€€) *(32 rue du Mont-Thabor, 1st, 01-42.60.82.52)*; you might spot Penelope Cruz there. Two doors away, **Le Soufflé (44)** (€€-€€€) *(36 rue du Mont-Thabor, 1st, 01-42.60.27.19)*, an American favorite, offers a large variety of sweet and

savory soufflés. Two streets down, quantity is the key word at **Lescure (45)** (€-€€) *(7 rue de Mondovi, 1st, 01-42.60.18.91)*, where the tables are so close together you can rub shoulders with your neighbor.

For soups, salads, and sandwiches, **Lunchtime (46)** (€) *(255 rue St-Honoré, 1st, 01-42.60.80.40)* hits the spot—and they do orders to go. Nearly around the corner, at **L'Écume St-Honoré (47)** (€-€€) *(6 rue du Marché-St-Honoré, 1st, 01-42.61.93.87)* you'll feel like you're in Brittany eating fresh oysters at a seaside shack. Communal wooden tables make brunch a rustic affair at **Le Pain Quotidien (48)** (€€) *(18 place du Marché-St-Honoré, 1st, 01-42.96.31.70)*. The cheese bar **Androuët Sur le Pouce (49)** (€) *(49 rue St-Roch, 1st, 01-42.97.57.39)* is great for lunch on the run and quiet dinners; it serves sandwiches, platters, and more. Splurge at **Le Carré des Feuillants (50)** (€€€) *(14 rue de Castiglione, 1st, 01-42.86.82.82)*, where the *haute cuisine* is fantastic and the service is superb. At least once, try the decadent desserts and rich hot chocolate at the old-world tea salon **Angelina (51)** (€) *(226 rue de Rivoli, 1st, 01-42.60.82.00)*.

One goes to **Café Marly (52)** (€€) *(93 rue de Rivoli, 1st, 01-49.26.06.60)*, facing I.M. Pei's pyramid, for its amazing setting and to see and be seen. The famous **Le Grand Véfour (53)** (€€€) *(17 rue de Beaujolais, 1st, 01-42.96.56.27)*, bordering the gardens of Palais Royal, is one of the most beautiful restaurants of Paris.

Mirrors reflect the Napoleonic splendor of elegant ceiling and wall paintings, sculpted cornices, and hanging light fixtures. It was frequented by Colette, Jean Cocteau, Victor Hugo, and Napoleon. To avoid paying an arm and a leg, try the prix-fixe lunch. For good value and a brasserie that seems like it hasn't changed in decades, **L'Épi d'Or (54)** (€-€€) *(25 rue Jean-Jacques Rousseau, 1st, 01-42.36.38.12)* has "French" stamped all over it; best to reserve for dinner and be on time. Great quality, inexpensive prices, and traditional cuisine make **Le Petit Flore (55)** (€) *(6 rue Croix des Petits Champs, 1st, 01-42.60.25.53)* hard to beat, but it's open for lunch only.

In the lavish **Galerie Vivienne (33)** near **Place des Victoires (35)** *(see also page 46)*, an indoor terrace with glass arcade gives warmth to the upscale tea salon **A Priori Thé (56)** (€€) *(35-37 Galerie Vivienne, 2nd, 01-42.97.48.75)*; it also serves weekend brunch. On the other side of **Place des Victoires (35)**, the trendy crowd flocks to the famous Parisian bistro **Chez Georges (57)** (€€-€€€) *(1 rue du Mail, 2nd, 01-42.60.07.11)* for an authentic experience of classic French food. Further north, across from the Bourse (old stock market), **Café Moderne (58)** (€€) *(40 rue Notre-Dame-des-Victoires, 2nd, 01-53.40.84.10)*—stylish, chic, yet cozy—boasts an eclectic menu with international flavors. Nearby, the draw at **Aux Lyonnais (59)** (€€-€€€) *(32 rue St-Marc, 2nd, 01-42.96.65.04)*, besides vintage bistro décor, is its owner, Alain Ducasse; the prices are very reasonable for Lyonnais cooking from this celebrated chef.

Bars & Nightlife:

Bar Hemingway (60) *(Hôtel Ritz, 15 pl. Vendôme, 1st, 01-43.16.33.65, www.ritzparis.com)*, made famous by its most illustrious client Papa H, might be a cliché but the wood and leather luxury exudes charm. **Le Café des Initiés (61)** *(3 pl. des Deux-Ecus, 1st, 01-42.33.78.29)* is a trendy *apéritif* hangout with friendly staff. For more elegance and a slightly colonial air, try **Le Fumoir (62)** *(6 rue de l'Amiral-de-Coligny, 1st, 01-42.92.00.24)*. Although **Le Pulp (63)** *(25 bd. Poissonnière, 2nd, 01-40.26.01.93, www.pulp-paris.com)* is an enormously popular and trendy lesbian club, it draws a mixed crowd on open nights: Wednesday and Thursday.

WHERE TO SHOP

Walk through the arches of the Rue de Rivoli, where boutiques and bookstores will catch your eye, including WH Smith (64) *(248 rue de Rivoli, 1st, 01-44.77.88.99, www.whsmith.fr)*, the renowned English bookseller. Across the Rue de Rivoli from the Louvre, the Louvre des Antiquaires (65) *(2 pl. du Palais-Royal, 1st, 01-42.97.27.27, www.louvre-antiquaires.com)* houses 250 reputable dealers of high-quality antiques.

Fine jewels are the theme at **Place Vendôme (31)** *(see also pages 45-46)*, where the great names of jewelry design sparkle with their gems: among them, Mauboussin (66) *(20 pl. Vendôme, 1st, 01-44.55.10.00)*, Van Cleef & Arpels (67) *(22 pl. Vendôme, 1st, 01-53.45.45.45, www.vancleef.com)*, Boucheron (68) *(26 pl. Vendôme, 1st, 01-42.61.58.16, www.boucheron.com)*, and Chanel (69) *(18 pl. Vendôme, 1st, 01-55.35.50.05, www.chanel.com)*. Fine

19th-century antique and Art Deco jewelry is typical at Faerber (71) *(12 rue de Castiglione, 1st, 01-44.50.50.44)*. Next door, for gems of another sort, take a whiff of jewelry designer Joel Rosenthal's exclusive perfumes at JAR (72) *(14 rue de Castiglione, 1st, 01-40.20.47.20)*. At the same address, sexy stilettos by Rodolphe Ménudier (73) *(14 rue de Castiglione, 1st, 01-42.60. 86.27)* are sure to turn heads. For classic men's shirts and pajamas, Charvet (74) *(28 pl. Vendôme, 1st, 01-42.60. 30.70)* has been shirtmaker to royalty and bourgeoisie since 1838.

Rue St-Honoré, just south of **Place Vendôme (31)** *(see also pages 45-46)*, is one of the most famous shopping streets of Paris. To the west it's called Rue du Faubourg-St-Honoré. As you walk eastward the shops go from extremely expensive couturiers to more moderate designer boutiques to the humbler shops of Les Halles. A few blocks east of Place Vendôme is an original Paris concept store, Colette (75) *(213 rue St-Honoré, 1st, 01-55.35.33.90)*, a design emporium of clothing, art objects, and electronics, with a photo gallery, bookshop, and exhibition space. Jacques Le Corre (76) *(193 rue St-Honoré, 1st, 01-42.96.97.40)* designs stylish but practical hats, bags, and shoes.

In the Palais Royal courtyard be sure to visit Italian costume jewelry designer Donatella Pellini (77) *(30 gal. de Montpensier, Jardins du Palais Royal, 1st, 01-42.96. 18.68)*, whose whimsical, elegant designs use stones and resins in cascades of colors and intriguing shapes. The destination for vintage haute couture is Didier Ludot (78) *(20-24 gal. de Montpensier, Jardins du Palais Royal, 1st, 01-42.96.06.56, www.didierludot.com)*. Alongside the Palais Royal, Martin Margiela (79) *(25 bis, rue de Montpensier, 1st, 01-40.15.07.55)*, protégé of Jean Paul Gaultier, has opened his own boutique of inventive clothing and accessories. At **Galerie Vivienne (33)** *(see also page 46)* you'll find stylish boutiques, such as Jean Paul Gaultier (80) *(No. 6, Galerie Vivienne, 1st)* and Christian Astuguevieille (81) *(No. 42, Galerie Vivienne, 1st)* with his furniture designs, sculpture, and drawings. Galerie Véro-Dodat (82) *(rue du Bouloi/Jean-Jacques Rousseau, 1st)* is another *passage* of antiquaries, vintage shops, and furniture designers.

Place des Victoires (35) *(see also page 46)* is the locus of major fashion boutiques, including Thierry Mugler (83) *(8 pl. des Victoires, 2nd)*, Kenzo (84) *(3 pl. des Victoires, 1st, 01-40.39.72.00)*, and Cacharel (85) *(pl. des Victoires, 1st/2nd)*. A street away, Sandrine Philippe (86) *(6 rue Hérold, 1st, 01-40.26.21.78)* designs sophisticated, romantic fashions with a way of making you feel like you're part of a story behind her clothes. Next door you'll find luxurious fabrics rich in color and texture at Dominique Kieffer (87) *(8 rue Hérold, 1st, 01-42.21.32. 44, www.dominiquekieffer.com)*, who creates textiles with a soul.

LES HALLES/MONTORGUEIL
HÔTEL DE VILLE/BEAUBOURG
MARAIS

Places to See:

1. Forum des Halles
2. Halles Garden
3. Fontaine des Innocents
4. Pavillon des Arts
5. St-Eustache
6. Bourse du Commerce
7. Tour Jean Sans Peur
8. Théâtre du Châtelet
49. Place du Châtelet
50. Théâtre de la Ville
51. Tour St-Jacques
52. Hôtel de Ville
53. St. Gervais-St. Protais
54. Cloître des Billettes
55. St-Merri
56. Centre Georges Pompidou
57. Fontaine de Stravinsky
58. Rue Quincampoix
59. 51 rue de Montmorency
60. IRCAM
61. Musée de la Poupée
62. Musée d'Art et d'Histoire du Judaïsme
63. L'Atelier de Fred
64. Musée des Arts et Métiers
84. Hôtel de Sens
85. Shoah Memorial
86. Rue des Rosiers
87. Hôtel de Sully
88. Place des Vosges
89. Victor Hugo House
90. Musée Carnavalet
91. Musée Cognacq-Jay
92. Picasso Museum
93. Hôtel de Rohan
94. Hôtel de Soubise
95. Rue Vieille-du-Temple
96. Rue Ste-Croix-de-la-Bretonnerie
97. Museum of Magic
98. Maison Européenne de la Photographie
99. La Galerie d'Architecture

Places to Eat & Drink:

9. Au Pied de Cochon
10. Restaurant Chez Max
11. Chez Denise—La Tour de Montlhéry
12. Le Père Fouettard
13. Au Chien qui Fume
14. Le Louchebem
15. La Victoire Suprème du Coeur
16. L'Ostréa

Where to Shop:

LES HALLES/MONTORGUEIL

4 *to Les Halles;* **1 4 7 11 14** *to Châtelet;*
7 *to Pont Neuf;* **1** *to Louvre-Rivoli;*
4 *to Étienne Marcel;*
3 *to Sentier;* **3 4** *to Réaumur-Sébastopol;*
4 8 9 *to Strasbourg-St-Denis*

● **SNAPSHOT** ●

Les Halles was once the farmers' market of Paris, shel-
tered beneath beautiful glass and cast-iron pavilions.
When Émile Zola dubbed it "the belly of Paris," he was
referring to the food market, but the description applied
equally to the unsavory and "alternate" characters who
inhabited the area. The pavilions were demolished in
1969 and were later replaced by the Forum des Halles,
an underground mall and transportation hub. A mixed
mass of humanity still crowds the streets, and Rue St-
Denis has long been a red-light district, but there are
plenty of remarkable spots in Les Halles. More picturesque, however, is the hip Montorgueil area, directly
north of the Forum. The small streets around Rue
Tiquetonne and Rue Étienne Marcel turn up funky cor-

ners and trendy finds. All-night
bistros thrive in Les Halles while
Montorgueil is crammed with
romantic cafés as well as food and
wine merchants slightly reminiscent of the old Halles.

PLACES TO SEE
Landmarks:

The **Forum des Halles (1)** *(Rues Rambuteau/Pierre Lescot/Berger, 1st)* is a three-level mall with shops, cinemas, and a pool. Despite its open central courtyard, it's rather gloomy. The surrounding landscape, the **Halles Garden (2)** *(west of Forum des Halles, 1st)*, is as devoid of charm as the Forum. Architecture and city planning buffs are challenged by this bad 1970s attempt at urban renewal. Kitty-corner (SE) from the Forum is the **Fontaine des Innocents (3)** *(Rue Berger/Rue Pierre Lescot, 1st)*, a Renaissance fountain erected on the site of the Innocents Cemetery, from which vast numbers of corpses were moved in 1785 to the Catacombs *(see Chapter 6, page 147)*. In the diametrically opposite corner of the Forum is a mushroom-shaped glass-and-steel structure, the **Pavillon des Arts (4)** *(101 rue Rambuteau, 1st, 01-42.33.82.50)*, an exhibition space.

Among this mishmash of futuristic bad taste is one of Paris's most magnificent churches, **St-Eustache (5)** *(Rue du Jour, 1st, 01-42.36.31.05, www.st-eustache.org)*, north of the **Halles Garden (2)** *(see also above)*. Modeled on Notre-Dame, with its flying buttresses, its plan is Gothic, but the decoration is sumptuously Renaissance. Historic figures are affiliated with this church, where Cardinal Richelieu and the Marquise de Pompadour (Louis XV's official mistress) were baptized. Another interesting building is nearby: at the east end of the **Halles Garden (2)**, the **Bourse du Commerce (6)** *(2 rue de Viarmes, 1st, 01-55.65.55.65)* provides group tours of this commodities market.

St-Eustache (5) *(see also page 59)* marks the beginning of a more soulful area north of Les Halles. Stroll along the narrow **Rue Montorgueil** and take in the flavors of the fruit and vegetable vendors, the wine and cheese merchants, and the ubiquitous cafés. The **Tour Jean Sans Peur (7)** *(20 rue Étienne Marcel, 2nd, 01-40.26.20.28, tour.jeansanspeur.free.fr)* was the Duke of Burgundy's attempt to protect himself from reprisals after he assassinated his rival, the Duke of Orleans, which was believed to have ignited the 100 Years' War. Burgundian symbols—oak, hawthorn, and hops—are carved into the turret. Rues Montorgueil, Tiquetonne, and Étienne Marcel are fun, funky places to explore around the Forum and are a bit more appealing to the eyes.

Arts & Entertainment:

The **Pavillon des Arts (4)** *(see also page 59)* exhibits unusual works, often showcasing unique objects or themes, from French as well as foreign museums. The free recitals at **St-Eustache (5)** (Sundays, 5:30 PM) *(see also page 59)* feature its 8,000-pipe organ. **Théâtre du Châtelet (8)** *(1 pl. du Châtelet, 1st, west side of the square, Info: 01-40.28.28.00, Booking: 01-40.28.28.41, www. chatelet-theatre.com)* is one of Paris's main venues for classical music, opera, and dance; its annual *Bleu sur Scène* blues festival brings major artists, like Herbie Hancock and Ornette Coleman.

PLACES TO EAT & DRINK
Where to Eat:

Though fast-food joints glut Les Halles, you can still eat well at a number of restaurants and cafés. A stone's throw from the **Bourse de Commerce (6)** *(see also page 59)* is a brasserie once frequented by market workers: **Au Pied de Cochon (9) (€-€€)** *(6 rue Coquillière, 1st, 01-40.13.77.00, open 24/7)* serves such classics as onion soup and oysters, but its specialty is grilled pig's feet in béarnaise sauce. You won't leave **Restaurant Chez Max (10) (€)** *(47 rue St-Honoré, 1st, 01-45.08.80.13, www.chez max.fr)* hungry—with its three-course meals, including a carafe of red or white wine—this is a great bargain. Several restaurants just south of Halles offer good deals. Fun, friendly, and open all night, **Chez Denise—La Tour de Montlhéry (11) (€€-€€€)** *(5 rue des Prouvaires, 1st, 01-42.36.21.82)* serves excellent classics and is frequented by artists, writers, and professional business "suits" alike. Inexpensive and relaxing, **Le Père Fouettard (12) (€)** *(9 rue Pierre Lescot, 1st, 01-42.33.74.17)* has a year-round terrace. **Au Chien qui Fume (13) (€-€€)** *(33 rue du Pont-Neuf, 1st, 01-42.36.07.42, www.au-chien-qui-fume.com)* serves delicious brasserie classics, including braised rabbit; the décor's motif is dogs dressed as people—the place is, after all, "The Smoking Dog."

Le Louchebem (14) (€-€€) *(31 rue Berger, 1st, 01-42.33.12.99, www.le-louchebem.fr)* is a steak lover's haven and another Halles original. Busiest at lunch, **La Victoire Suprême du Coeur (15) (€)** *(41 rue des Bourdonnais, 1st,*

01-40.41.93.95) is a vegetarian restaurant that caters to those with "health" on the mind. Excellent fresh fish is the specialty at **L'Ostréa (16)** **(€€-€€€)** *(4 rue Sauval, 1st, 01-40.26.08.07)*.

In the Montorgueil area, **La Potée des Halles (17)** **(€-€€)** *(3 rue Étienne Marcel, 1st, 01-40.41.98.15)* is steamy with beans, cabbage, pork, and veal. Classified a national monument, its tiled walls depict hand-painted beer and coffee goddesses. The original chairs display the names of Halles workers who were regulars; some of them still are, at 70 or 80. Another authentic working-class haunt, **Le Cochon à l'Oreille (18)** **(€)** *(15 rue Montmartre, 1st, 01-42.36.07.56)* serves huge, hearty portions to a mostly French clientele. In the lively food market street, Rue Montorgueil, from which the area gets its name, **Foody's Brunch Café (19)** **(€)** *(26 rue Montorgueil, 1st, 01-40.13.02.53)* is a self-service vegetarian restaurant with soups, salads, fresh juice, and bakery goods at great prices. Artistry and imagination are bywords at **Aux Trois Petits Cochons (20)** **(€-€€)** *(31 rue Tiquetonne, 2nd, 01-42.33.39.69, www.auxtroispetitscochons.fr, dinner only)*, where the food is noteworthy and the presentation carefully arranged. The owners' success led to a second restaurant a street away: more informal, **Pig'z (21)** **(€€)** *(5 rue Marie Stuart, 2nd, 01-42.33.05.89, www.pigz.fr,*

dinner only) is just as popular, so reserve a table. You'll get a shot of local neighbors and artists at both places. The oldest *pâtisserie* in Paris, classified as a historical monument, **Stohrer (22)** (€) *(51 rue Montorgueil, 2nd, 01-42.33.38.20, www.stohrer.fr)* was opened in 1730 by Marie Antoinette's personal baker. Now we know why she said, "Let them eat cake!" Around the corner, at the classic, old-style bistro **Aux Crus de Bourgogne (23)** (€€) *(3 rue Bachaumont, 2nd, 01-42.33.48.24)* nostalgia is served up with the house specialty, fresh lobster. **La Crêpe Dentelle (30)** (€) *(10 rue Léopold Bellan, 2nd, 01-40.41.04.23)* is a family-run *crêperie* serving an array of delicious crêpes and indulgent desserts.

Bars & Nightlife:

Kong (24) *(1 rue du Pont-Neuf, 1st, 01-40.39.09.00)* is one of the city's hot spots designed by hotshot Philippe Starck and featured on *Sex and the City*—the too-too-cool staff is part of the heavy-on-style, light-on-substance ambience. One of the most famous jazz clubs in Europe is **Le Slow Club (25)** *(130 rue de Rivoli, 1st, 01-42.33.84.30)*, with big band and R&B rocking the tiny space. **Rue des Lombards** in Les Halles is known for live jazz. Among the notable clubs of the street are **Au Duc des Lombards (26)** *(42 rue des Lombards, 1st, 01-42.33.22.88)*, and **Baiser Salé (27)** *(58 rue des Lombards, 1st, 01-42.33.37.71)*. Included in the list is also **Le Sunset/Le Sunside (28)** *(60 rue des Lombards, 1st, 01-40.26.21.25, www.sunset-sunside.com)*, where artists from both sides of the Atlantic play (electric in the former; acoustic, the latter). Lively **Bistrot d'Eustache (29)** (€-€€) *(37 rue Berger, 1st, 01-40.26.23.20)*, a

charming throwback to the jazz age of the 1930s and 1940s, serves traditional French food; the jazz is live, with gypsy guitar jazz on Thursday nights.

WHERE TO SHOP

La Grande Boutique de l'Artisan Parfumeur (31) *(2 rue l'Amiral Coligny, 1st, 01-44.88.27.50, www.laboutiquedelartisanparfumeur.com)* is the flagship store of the grand perfume specialist. Besides selling fragrances, candles, and creams, the place gives evening lectures on the art and history of perfumery. With clothing by up-and-coming avant-garde designers, grafitti-filled walls, and photo exhibits, Surface to Air Boutique (32) *(46 rue l'Arbre Sec, 1st, 01-44.27.04.54, www.surface2air.com)* is the cat's meow in concept stores. If you must take home an enamel Parisian street sign, go to Papeterie Moderne (33) *(12 rue de la Ferronnerie, 1st, 01-42.36.21.72)*.

Hop to the other side of Les Halles for all manner of kitchen utensils and tableware at the famous E. Dehillerin (34) *(18 rue Coquillière, 1st, 01-42.36.53.13)*. The competition is equally famous: A. Simon (35) *(48 rue Montmartre, 2nd, 01-42.33.71.65)* and Mora (36) *(13 rue Montmartre, 1st, 01-45.08.19.24)*. For all manner of beads, ribbon, buttons, yarn, and trim, visit La Droguerie (37) *(9-11 rue du Jour, 1st, 01-45.08.93.27)*. Rue du Jour has spawned a small Agnès b (38) *(2, 3, 6, 10, 19 rue du*

Jour, 1st; Women: 01-45.08.56.56, Men: 01-42.33.04.13, www.agnesb.fr) empire where black is the staple wardrobe color and some bright patterns are mixed in for fun. For the little black beret, little black suit, little black cardigan, head to Claudie Pierlot (39) *(1 rue Montmartre, 1st, 01-42.21.38.38)*.

When the walking gets to you, enter the medieval stone walls of Spa Nuxe (40) *(32 rue Montorgueil, 1st, 01-55.80.71.40, www.nuxe.com)* for an exotic serene experience of their treatments, or just pick up a few beauty products. Conversely, try the hammam (Turkish bath) at Aux Bains Montorgueil (41) *(55 rue Montorgueil, 2nd, 01-44.88.01.78)* for a steam bath, exfoliation, and massage. If sewing and crafts are your passion, don't miss Declercq Passementiers (42) *(15 rue Étienne Marcel, 1st, 01-44.76.90.70, www.declercqpassementiers.fr)* for fantastic trimmings and tassels. Walk along the trendy **Rue Étienne Marcel**, lined with hip names in fashion—Yohji Yamamoto, Joseph, and Diesel, among others. In the Montorgueil quarter, **Rue Tiquetonne** is a trendsetter. It's full of workshops, restaurants, and boutiques, including Killiwatch (43) *(64 rue Tiquetonne, 2nd, 01-42.21. 17.37)*, a designer and secondhand clothing store. Increasingly popular, it sells used fashions by the kilo. Next door, the elegant, sexy, and feminine shoes at Patrick Cox (44) *(62 rue Tiquetonne, 2nd, 01-40. 26.66.55)* practically strut off the catwalk. One street up, between rue St-Denis and rue Dussoubs is the Passage du Grand Cerf (45) *(St-Denis/Rue Dussoubs)*, with its Belle Époque ironwork and funky, fashionable shops of clothing, accessory, lighting, and art objects; a few prominent ones are **Ghislaine du Tertre** (No. 1) for your wool and knit enthusiasts, **As'Art** (No. 3) for unique African and ethnic gifts, and **Johanna Braitbart** (No. 8) to satisfy your vintage jewelry and accessories cravings. Barbara Bui (46) *(23 rue Etienne Marcel, 2nd, 01-40.26.43.65, www.barbarabui.com)* reflects her French and Vietnamese roots with refined and graceful designer clothes.

WHERE TO STAY

Les Halles isn't the best place to stay, but the Montorgueil area affords some bargains. Ambience is missing at the **Tiquetonne Hotel (47)** (€) *(6 rue Tiquetonne, 2nd, 01-42.36.94.58)* but it's cheap, clean, and very, very basic (with chenille bedspreads). **Hôtel du Cygne (48)** (€) *(3 rue du Cygne, 1st, 01-42.60.14.16, www.hotelducygne.fr)* is reliable, appealing, and livable, with rooms decorated in Laura Ashley style.

HÔTEL DE VILLE/BEAUBOURG

①④⑦⑪⑭ *to Châtelet;*
①⑪ *to Hôtel de Ville;* **⑪** *to Rambuteau;*
③⑪ *to Arts et Métiers;*
③④ *to Réaumur-Sébastopol;*
④⑧⑨ *to Strasbourg-St-Denis*

● SNAPSHOT ●

Dominated by the Hôtel de Ville (town hall) and the Centre Georges Pompidou (colloquially referred to as "Beaubourg"), this district is jam-packed with interesting landmarks, museums, bars, and shops. Two aesthetics coexist: the ornate marble—replete with turrets and statues—of the Hôtel de Ville corresponds to the pomp and circumstance of its stature; a few streets away the "inside-out" structure of Beaubourg—with color-coded pipes, scaffolding, and ducts—puts the functional works of the building on public display. The district is exciting and vibrant, attracting a crowd eager for street spectacles—and there are plenty of those in the Hôtel de Ville/Beaubourg quarter.

PLACES TO SEE
Landmarks:

Start at **Place du Châtelet (49)** *(at bd. De Sébastopol, 4th)*, which was once a fortress defending the city from the north and is now a major métro hub. Aboveground, in the center of the square is a fountain—yet another monument to Napoleon's victories. On either side of

Place du Châtelet (49) are the twin theaters **Théâtre du Châtelet (8)** *(west side; see page 60)* and **Théâtre de la Ville (50)** *(east side; 2 pl. du Châtelet, 4th, 01-42.74.22.77, www.theatredelaville-paris.com)*. In the NE corner, the **Tour St-Jacques (51)** *(Sq. de la Tour St-Jacques, 4th)* seems to oversee the area. Flamboyantly Gothic, the tower is what is left standing of a church that served as the meeting point for pilgrims before venturing out on voyages. The tower was a favorite of the Surrealists, perhaps because of the plethora of gargoyles or because of their incongruity with the figure at the base of the tower, a statue of Blaise Pascal, who conducted barometrical experiments at the site in the 17th century.

As you walk along the *quai* (embankment) of the Seine eastward, gaze along the river at the fabulous views. Across the Seine, you'll see the old **Conciergerie** prison *(see Chapter 5, page 114)*; further to the left, the cathedral of **Notre-Dame** *(see Chapter 5, page 114)*; and in the distance to the right, the **Eiffel Tower** *(see Chapter 1, page 22)*. Great photo ops! Continuing along the *quai*, you'll arrive at the **Hôtel de Ville (52)** *(Pl. de l'Hôtel de Ville, 29 rue de Rivoli, 4th, 01-42.76.43.43)*, which serves as town

hall, city council premises, and official residence of the mayor of Paris. It is also the venue for receptions honoring foreign dignitaries. With its elaborate, sculpted exterior and the impressive interior adorned with chandeliers, statues, caryatids, and a majestic staircase, the **Hôtel de Ville (52)** exudes power, pomp, and ceremony. The square facing the building has had its share of power-filled days: it was once the main site for public executions.

East of the **Hôtel de Ville (52)** is the 6th-century church **St. Gervais-St. Protais (53)** *(Pl. St-Gervais, 4th, 01.48.87.32.02)*, the façade of which is made up of three levels of columns—Doric, Ionic, and Corinthian. This beautiful church is famous for its lovely religious music. Walk around the back, up the picturesque **Rue des Barres** where artists set up their easels and small cafés cover the terraced sidewalk with tables and chairs. A few streets north-westward is the 7th-century church of **St-Merri (55)** *(76 rue de la Verrerie, 4th, 01-42.71.93.93)*, decidedly Gothic.

Follow the Rue St-Martin two streets north and you'll come to the **Centre Georges Pompidou (56)**, or "Beaubourg" *(Rue Beaubourg, 4th, 01-44.78.12.33, www.centrepompidou.fr)*. Opened in 1977, it was an immediate success and has remained so; its inside-out structure makes it one of the most unique examples of modern architecture. The workings of the building—air ducts, water shafts, utility pipes, elevators, escalators, and structural steel struts—are all on the outside, color-coded to distinguish their functions, while the glass and steel walls give a sense of interior-exterior permeability. This leaves the entire interior space with the flexibility to adapt to the center's activities and needs. The museum boasts a collection of more than 50,000 works covering painting, sculpture, drawing, photography, architecture, design, cinema, video, and audio-visual archives in addition to a library, screening rooms, and performance and exhibition spaces.

Outside Beaubourg, on the large esplanade, pavement artists and street performers do their thing to crowds of willing onlookers. South of Beaubourg, the **Fontaine de Stravinsky (57)** *(Pl. Igor Stravinsky, rue Brismiche, 4th)*, created by artists Niki de St-Phalle and Jean Tinguély, is an intermingling orchestra of delightfully colorful and fanciful creature sculptures, each contributing to the waterworks extravaganza. Along **Rue Quincampoix (58)** *(Rue des Lombards/Rue Rambuteau, 4th)*, a bevy of galleries, cafés, and bars animate the cobblestone street and its restored 18th-century residences. A block past its northern end is the (probably) oldest house in Paris: **51 rue de Montmorency (59)** *(Rue Beaubourg/Rue St-Martin, 3rd)* built in 1407.

Arts & Entertainment:

Théâtre de la Ville (50) *(see also page 68)* is a must-stop for modern dance fans, where many important choreographers, such as Maguy Marin and Jean-Claude Gallotta, have showcased their talents. The modern art exhibits, audio-visual screenings, and performance art at **Centre Georges Pompidou (56)** *(see also page 69)* are not to be missed. By the southern flank of Centre Pompidou,

IRCAM (60) *(1 pl. Igor Stravinsky, 4th, 01-44.78.48.43)*, dedicated to musical experimentation and research, offers contemporary music concerts; Pierre Boulez has been actively involved in IRCAM since its conception. A street north of Beaubourg, the **Musée de la Poupée (61)** *(Impasse Berthaud, 3rd, 01-42.72.73.11)* exhibits dolls from around the world, has a doll hospital, and offers doll-making classes for adults and children. The **Musée d'Art et d'Histoire du Judaïsme (62)** *(Hôtel de St-Aignan, 71 rue du Temple, 3rd, 01-53.01.86.60)* is dedicated to French Jewish culture from the Middle Ages to the present. Take cooking classes (small groups) at **L'Atelier de Fred (63)** *(6 rue des Vertus, 3rd, 01-40.29.46.04, www.latelierdefred.com)* to impress your friends back home with an authentic, homemade Parisian meal. The **Musée des Arts et Métiers (64)** *(Museum of Science and Industry) (60 rue Réaumur, 3rd, 01-53.01.82.00, www. arts-and-metiers.net)* hosts conferences ranging from Walkman technology to how to anticipate natural disasters; among other inventive objects, the mechanical figures and prototype machines are amusing.

PLACES TO EAT & DRINK
Where to Eat:

Take in the sights, from the fashion-model wait staff to the Parisian rooftops and major gems of the city, at **Georges (67)** (€€-€€€) *(Centre Pompidou, 19 rue Beaubourg, 4th, 01-44.78.47.99)*, the ultra-chic café-restaurant on the terrace of Beaubourg; the food's good and the view is superlative. Best for drinks, light fare, and brunch, **Café Beaubourg (68)** (€€) *(100 rue St-Martin, 4th, 01-48.87.63.96)* faces the esplanade of

Beaubourg—and offers its fashionable patrons a great place from which to people-watch. For classic French dishes that are simple but surprising, **Le Hangar (69)** (€€) *(12 impasse Berthaud, 3rd, 01-42.74.55.44, cash only)*, a cozy bistro by the doll museum, is one of the best values in Paris. Around the corner is another great find: good food and friendly staff are served up at **Le Petit Marcel (70)** (€) *(65 rue Rambuteau, 4th, 01-48.87.10.20)*. **Le 404 (71)** (€€) *(69 rue des Gravilliers, 3rd, 01-42.74.57.81)* is a fabulous Moroccan restaurant that's funky, sexy, and noisy; get down with the table-dancing crowd.

Bars & Nightlife:

Andy Wahloo (73) *(69 rue Gravilliers, 3rd, 01-42.71.20.38)*, a North African bar next door to **Le 404 (71)** *(see above)*, has an industrial décor and amicable staff ready to serve beer, cocktails, and hookahs.

PLACES TO SEE
Landmarks:

Just past the **Pont-Marie** and one street in from the river, **Hôtel de Sens (84)** *(1 rue du Figuier, 4th, 01-42.78. 14.60)*, now home to the Forney fine arts library, is a rare medieval building built between 1475-1507, its turrets and arches evocative of a time when Bourbons, Guises, and Cardinal de Pellevé occupied the premises. Just westward, at the border of the Jewish quarter, the **Shoah Memorial (85)** *(17 rue Geoffroy-l'Asnier, 4th, 01-42.77.44.72)*, with its Memorial to the Unknown Jewish Martyr, is a memorial, study center, and museum dedicated to the Holocaust. The heart of the Jewish quarter is **Rue des Rosiers (86)** *(Rue Vielle du Temple/Rue Malher, 4th)*, a colorful area full of delis, bakeries, and falafel shops alongside synagogues. The **Hôtel de Sully (87)** *(62 rue St-Antoine, 4th, 01-44.61.20.00)*, a beautiful late-Renaissance mansion, houses the Center for National Monuments.

A step away is the heart of the Marais, the **Place des Vosges (88)** *(Rue des Francs Bourgeois, 4th)*. Perhaps the most lovely and aesthetically pleasing square in the world, it's perfectly symmetrical: 36 houses, equally placed on four sides, stand gracefully over rows of arcades. Red brick and stone facades with slate blue roofs and dormer windows lend a simple yet regal elegance to the large square, where jousts, tournaments, and historic

events took place. Literati, such as Madame de Sévigné, held salons here. The **Victor Hugo House (89)** *(6 pl. des Vosges, 4th, 01-42.72.10.16)* is where the writer lived; and where *Les Misérables* was created. Stroll under the arcades to find a variety of shops, galleries, and cafés— it's where Inspector Maigret of the Simenon detective novels likes to sip a *café-au-lait*.

Explore the many stunning small streets in the area as you make your way northward toward the **Musée Carnavalet (90)** *(23 rue de Sévigné, 3rd, 01-44.59.58.58)*, a mansion dedicated to the history of Paris *(see also page 77)*. One street westward, you have the opportunity to enter an old Marais home: the **Musée Cognacq-Jay (91)** *(Hôtel de Donon, 8 rue Elzévir, 4th, 01-40.27.07.21)* was once the residence of a prominent businessman and art collector. A short walk away, the **Picasso Museum (92)** *(Hôtel Salé, 5 rue de Thorigny, 3rd, 01-42.71.25.21, www.musee-picasso.fr)* is housed in a grand Marais mansion. Picasso admirers are treated to masterpieces in paintings, etchings, and sculptures. Kitty-corner, the

National Archives are housed in the **Hôtel de Rohan (93)** *(87 rue Vieille-du-Temple, 3rd, 01-40.27.60.09)* and around the corner in the **Hôtel de Soubise (94)** *(60 rue des Francs-Bourgeois, 3rd, 01-40.27.60.96)*; both buildings are marvelous examples of 18th-century architecture. **Cloître des Billettes (54)** *(24 rue des Archives, 4th, 01-40.72.38.79)*, the oldest medieval cloister in Paris was built in 1427 for the Brothers of Charity. The courtyard, with its Gothic galleries, colonnaded arches, and arcades topped by graceful vaults, is especially appealing. The cloister presents work by emerging artists; exhibits change twice a month and are usually free. Be sure to stroll along the **Rue Vieille-du-Temple (95)** *(Rue de Rivoli/Rue de Poitou, 3rd/4th)*—its charm comes not only from the 13th-century medieval houses but also from the street's many luxury shops. Further to the west, around **Rue Ste-Croix-de-la-Bretonnerie (96)** *(Rue de Temple/Rue Vielle de Temple, 4th)*, is the **gay district** ("pink triangle"), a vibrant, stylish scene replete with hotels, bars, clubs, and restaurants.

Arts & Entertainment:

Magicians ply their trade outside the wonderful **Museum of Magic (97)** *(11 rue St-Paul, 4th, 01-42.72.13.26, www.museedelamagie.com)*; inside, they demonstrate with museum pieces. In a magnificent mansion, the **Maison Européenne de la Photographie (98)** *(5-7 rue de Fourcy, 4th, 01-44.78.75.00, www.mep-fr.org)* houses more than 15,000 works of contemporary photography; and its café is super-chic. The 140-room **Musée Carnavalet (90)** *(see also page 76)* covers the history of Paris, through paintings, sculptures, documents, objects, and memorabilia. Some samplings of what is on view are: a piece of the Bastille prison, lithographs, porcelain vases, and Proust's reconstructed cork-lined bedroom (where he wrote most of *A la recherche du temps perdu, Remembrance of Things Past*). On a more human scale, the refined **Musée Cognacq-Jay (91)** *(see also page 76)* is home to a once private collection of 18th-century art and furniture. The **Picasso Museum (92)** *(see also page 76)* has an astonishing collection of work from all periods of the artist's long and diverse career. **La Galerie d'Architecture (99)** *(11 rue des Blancs-Manteaux, 4th, 01-49.96.64.00, www.galerie-architecture.fr)* shows the work of contemporary architects against a clean, crisp, white backdrop.

PLACES TO EAT & DRINK
Where to Eat:
Supposedly the first wine bar in Paris, **Le Coude Fou (65)** **(€€)** *(12 rue du Bourg-Tibourg, 4th, 01-42.77.15.16)* is friendly and intimate with food better than the usual wine bar fare. The best afternoon tea outside London is to be had at **Mariage Frères (66)** **(€€)** *(30 rue du Bourg-Tibourg, 4th, 01-42.72.28.11)*. A gem of haute cuisine, **L'Ambroisie (100)** **(€€€)** *(9 pl. des Vosges, 4th, 01-42.78.51.45)* is said to be one of the most beautiful restaurants in Paris. The food is spectacular while the décor is ornate and Versailles-like; the unique experience is worth the steep price. For a less refined evening, **L'Auberge de Jarente (101)** **(€)** *(7 rue Jarente, 4th, 01-42.77.49.35)* is casual, friendly, and serves hearty Basque food. At **Au Bourguignon du Marais (102)** **(€€)** *(52 rue François-Miron, 4th, 01-48.87.15.40)* the excellent selection of Burgundy goes with its classic bistro fare. **Piccolo Teatro (103)** **(€)** *(6 rue des Écouffes, 4th, 01-42.72.17.79)* is a charming vegetarian restaurant serving

up international dishes (including organic soups) amid the stone wall and wooden beam setting. **Rue des Rosiers (86)** is the locus for Jewish delis, the most famous being **Jo Goldenberg (104)** (€) *(7 rue des Rosiers, 4th, 01-48.87.20.16)*. Best for cakes and tea, **Le Loir dans la Théière (105)** (€) *(3 rue des Rosiers, 4th, 01-42.72.90.61)* is funky and cool. Senegalese and African dishes and delicacies are on the menu at **Le Petit Dakar (106)** (€) *(6 rue Elzévir, 3rd, 01-44.59.34.74, www.csao. fr)*. Several blocks north of the **Picasso Museum (92)**, in a simple, uncluttered interior, the menu at **R'Aliment (107)** (€-€€) *(57 rue Charlot, 3rd, 01-48.04.88.28)* favors organic products and vegetarian dishes. For arguably the best couscous in Paris, try **Chez Omar (108)** (€-€€) *(47 rue de Bretagne, 3rd, 01-42.72.36.26)*, a North African favorite among the cognoscenti and trendy patrons.

Bars & Nightlife:

You might expect Edith Piaf to saunter into **Le Connétable (72)** *(55 rue des Archives, 3rd, 01-42.77. 41.40)*: it's a typical Parisian bar, chatty regulars and all. Vibrant sounds in music—from cabaret to jazz to fusion—emanate from **Les 7 Lézards (109)** *(10 rue des Rosiers, 4th, 01-48.87.08.97, www.7 lezards.com)*. **Le Jokko (110)** *(5 rue Elzévir, 3rd, 01-42.74.35.96, www. csao.fr)* is an African-themed bar and exhibition space featuring live music. At the literary wine bar **La**

Belle Hortense (111) *(31 rue Vieille-du-Temple, 4th, 01-48.04.71.60, www.cafeine.com)*, sip a glass of red wine and peruse a book from the window ledges. For some, wine's a game; at **L'Apparement (112)** *(18 rue des Coutures-St-Gervais, 3rd, 01-48.87.12.22)* wine *goes with* the game: you can play cards or a board game while sipping your *verre de rouge*. Further south in the **gay district**, (also known as the "pink triangle"), **L'Open Café (113)** *(17 rue des Archives, 4th, 01-42.72.26.18)* is a favorite gay café and a happening night spot. Mixed gay-straight techno-lovers crowd the floor of **Le Mixer (114)** *(23 rue Ste-Croix-de-la-Bretonnerie, 4th, 01-48.87.55.44)*. Straight-friendly gay locale **Amnésia Café (115)** *(42 rue Vieille-du-Temple, 4th, 01-42.72.16.94)* gets rowdy at night; they serve drinks, sandwiches, and brunch. Nearby, long-standing **Le Central (116)** *(33 rue Vieille-du-Temple, 4th, 01-48.87.99.33)* is a cozy spot for natives and travelers alike.

WHERE TO SHOP

Julian Schnabel's art adorns the walls of the showroom loft of Tunisian-born Azzedine Alaïa (77) *(7 rue de Moussy, 4th, 01-42.72.19.19)*, emphasizing that the sexy, form-fitting clothes are wearable art. Colorful tweeds and woolens, Audrey Hepburn-style, make Blancs Manteaux (78) *(42 rue des Blancs Manteaux, 4th, 01-42.71.00.00)* a find; its wares are mostly shipped, so the shop is more of a depot. Stroll through the 60 or so shops of antiques and bric-a-brac dealers at Village St-Paul (117) *(14-15 rue St-Paul, near rue Charlemagne, 4th)*. The handmade leather goods at Serge Amoruso

(118) *(39 rue du Roi-de-Sicile, 4th, 01-48.04.97.97)* are a labor of love; watch the artisans as they perform magic in the workshop. Across the street, the original designs of Korean-American Kyungmee J. (119) *(38 rue du Roi-de-Sicile, 4th, 01-42.74.33.85)*, elegantly asymmetrical with unusual mixes of patterns and colors, appeal to artists, dancers, and architects. Fun, coquettish clothes are the look at Lolita Lempicka (120) *(13 bis, rue Pavée, 4th, 01-42.74.50.48)*, with half-price end-of-line items around the corner at Studio Lolita (121) *(2 bis, rue des Rosiers, 4th, 01-48.87.09.67)*.

Rue des Francs-Bourgeois is a great shopping street. Fabulous white linen and stretchy laces are elegant and comfortable at Anne Fontaine (122) *(12 rue des Francs-Bourgeois, 3rd, 01-44.59.81.59)*. Enter Ali Baba's cave, full of fabulous Tunisian homeware, at 2 Mille et 1 Nuits (123) *(13 rue des Francs-Bourgeois, 4th, 01-48.87.07.07, www.2001nuits.com)*. Down the street, Paris-Musées (124) *(29 bis rue des Francs-Bourgeois, 4th, 01-42.74. 13.02)* features reproductions from Parisian museums and other home accents. Zadig & Voltaire (125) *(42 rue des Francs-Bourgeois, 3rd, 01-44.54.00.60, www.zadig-et-voltaire.com)*, with branches around the city, is popular for its casual, urban wardrobe offerings. Issey Miyake's innovative textile design is evident at A-poc (126) *(47 rue des Francs-Bourgeois, 4th, 01-44. 54.07.05, www.isseymiyake.com)*; the name is derived from "a piece of cloth," the concept being to design wearable art from one piece of fabric.

Painted chests and armoires abound among the refurbished 18th- and 19th-century furniture at Meubles Peints (127) *(32 rue Sévigné, 4th, 01-42.77.54.60, www.meublespeints.com)*. Photo buffs will flock to fashion photography bookshop Comptoir de l'Image (128) *(44 rue de Sévigné, 3rd, 01-42.72.03.92)* and Galerie Chez Valentin (129) *(9 rue St-Gilles, 3rd, 01-48.87.42.55)*, which exhibits experimental video, photography, and installations. African art and crafts are on display at La Boutique (130) *(1-3 rue Elzévir, 3rd, 01-44.54.55.88, www.csao.fr)*, and contemporary African art shows a few doors away at La Galerie 3A (131) *(15-17 rue Elzévir, 3rd, www.csao.fr)*. Wispy fabrics, inventive details, and incredible use of color have given the Japanese fashion designer Tsumori Chisato (132) *(20 rue Barbette, 3rd, 01-42.78.18.88)* a dedicated fan base in Paris. The Bains du Marais (133) *(31-33 rue des Blancs-Manteaux, 4th, 01-44.61.02.02, www.lesbainsdu marais.com)* offers a break from the wear and tear of sightseeing and shopping. Open to women Monday–Wednesday, men Thursday–Saturday, and both on weekends, the spa gives divine hammam treatments; or combine a facial with manicure, pedicure, haircut, and other salon offerings.

Rue Vieille-du-Temple (95) is another treasure trove for shopping. Tapestries and cushions, reproductions of those found in the Cluny Museum and the Louvre, are handmade at Artis Flora (134) *(75 rue Vieille-du-Temple, 3rd, 01-48.87.76.18)*. Limited-edition designer tableware gives new meaning to glassware and crockery at Chône (135) *(60 rue Vieille-du-Temple, 3rd, 01-44.78.90.00)*. Chocolates and pastries reign at Cacao et Chocolat (136) *(36 rue Vieille-du-Temple, 4th, 01-42.71.50.06)*. Make a style statement at Le Mouton à Cinq Pattes (137) *(15 rue Vieille-du-Temple, 4th, 01-42.71.86.30)* with its great buys in vintage designer clothes and pieces from last season's collections.

For carefully crafted books on international architecture, art, and design, try Archibooks (138) *(18-20 rue de la Perle, 3rd, 01-42.25.15.58, www.archibooks.com)*. A few streets up from the Picasso Museum (92) *(see also page 76)*, find fine ceramics and porcelain at Galerie Pierre (139) *(22 rue Debelleyme, 3rd, 01-42.72.20.24)*. Hunt for great discounts at L'Habilleur (140) *(44 rue de Poitou, 3rd, 01-48.87.77.12)*: end-of-line designer pieces and hot-off-the-runway creations are 50%-70% off. Rue Charlot (141) *(beginning at rue des Quatre Fils, 3rd)* has been inventively redone, harboring galleries, bookshops, cafés, and shops, such as **Passage de Retz** (No. 9), **Food** (No. 58), and **Moon Young Hee** (No. 62).

WHERE TO STAY

Haute couture designer Azzedine Alaïa's **3 Rooms (80)** (€€€) *(5 rue de Moussy, 4th, 01-44.78.92.00, www.3rooms-10corsocomo.com)* equals minimalist chic, with lighting and furniture by international designers; the price is equally *haut*. A street away **Hôtel Bourg Tibourg (81)** (€€-€€€) *(19 rue du Bourg-Tibourg, 4th, 01-42.78.47.39, www.hotelbourgtibourg.com)*—part of the Costes Brothers' empire—is dramatic, sensual, and intimate; silk and taffeta, fringes and tassels, the hotel is a tasteful combination of styles, textures, and colors reminiscent of the private inner chambers of a princely retreat. A revamped 17th-century townhouse, **Hôtel de la Bretonnerie (82)** (€-€€) *(22 rue Ste-Croix-de-la-Bretonnerie, 4th, 01-48.87.77.63, www.bretonnerie.com)* is comfortable, tasteful, and a good value. In the budget category, **Hôtel de Nice (83)** (€) *(42 bis, rue de Rivoli, 4th, 01-42.78.55.29)* is filled with "busy" patterns and textiles and has its space challenges, but is a good bargain and is well located.

Near the Jewish quarter at the **Hôtel Caron de Beaumarchais (142)** (€€) *(12 rue Vieille-du-Temple, 4th, 01-42.72.34.12, www.carondebeaumarchais.com)* the service is impeccable; small rooms with 18th-century décor are prepared with great attention to detail. A good find at a reasonable price (especially for the neighborhood), **Grand Hôtel Malher (143)** (€-€€) *(5 rue Malher, 4th, 01-42.72.60.92, www.grandhotelmalher.com)* is comfortable and well run. Simple and unassuming, **Grand Hôtel Jeanne d'Arc (144)** (€) *(3 rue Jarente, 4th,*

BASTILLE
CANAL ST-MARTIN

Places to See:

1. Place de la Bastille
2. Colonne de Juillet
3. Opéra Bastille
4. Marché d'Aligre
5. Pavillon de l'Arsenal
32. Rue du Faubourg-du-Temple
33. St-Louis Hospital
34. Port de l'Arsenal

Places to Eat & Drink:

6. Le Train Bleu
7. Le Viaduc Café
8. Le Square Trousseau
9. Le China Club
10. Ramulaud
11. Le Temps au Temps
12. L'Ecailler du Bistrot
13. Bistrot Paul Bert
14. Le Vieux Chêne
15. Pause Café
16. Le Souk
17. Au C'Amelot
18. Le Balajo
19. Le Café du Passage
20. La Muse Vin
21. LeWax

22. Café de l'Industrie
35. Chez Prune
36. La Marine
37. Favela Chic
38. Hôtel du Nord
39. Le Villaret
40. Le Verre Volé
41. L'Atmosphère
42. Le Vin de Zinc

Where to Shop:

23. Viaduc des Arts
24. Isabel Marant
25. Gaëlle Barré
26. Anne Willi
27. Come On Eileen
43. Artazart
44. Stella Cadente
45. Antoine et Lili

Where to Stay:

28. Hôtel Lyon-Mulhouse
29. Daval Hôtel
30. Hôtel le Pavillon Bastille
31. Centre Parisien de Zen
46. Hôtel Notre-Dame
47. Hôtel Plessis
48. Hôtel de Nevers

BASTILLE

1 **5** **8** *to Bastille;* **8** *to Ledru-Rollin;*
1 **⑭** *to Gare de Lyon;* **5** **9** *to Oberkampf*

• SNAPSHOT •

The Bastille prison stormed by the people on July 14, 1789, during the French Revolution, no longer exists, though pieces of it can be seen in the Musée Carnavalet *(see Chapter 3, pages 76-77)*. However, its ghosts seem to hover over the quarter, reminding us of the power of the people. The Place de la Bastille became a marker dividing central Paris from the working-class neighborhoods in the eastern part of the city. Recently gentrified, the Bastille district has become a center of activity, from the Opéra Bastille to the burgeoning cafés and shops. Bistros and restaurants abound; many retain their working-class flavor with a twist while others bring in a new air.

PLACES TO SEE
Landmarks:

The French Revolution was followed decades later by other revolts. To commemorate those killed during the uprisings of 1830 and 1848, a bronze column was

erected in the center of the **Place de la Bastille (1)** *(Bd. Beaumarchais/Rue du Faubourg, 4th)*: the **Colonne de Juillet (2)** *(Pl. de la Bastille, 4th)* bears the names of many buried in the crypt beneath the column. At its apex is the statue "The Genius of Liberty." The **Opéra Bastille (3)** *(120 rue de Lyon, 12th, 01-72.29.35.35, www.operadeparis.fr)*, officially opened by President Mitterand on Bastille Day 1989 as part of the celebrations of the Bicentennial of the French Revolution, is as far removed from the Opéra Garnier as imaginable yet still retains a majesty of its own. The façade is glass while the interior is granite with an amazing glass ceiling. A feat of technological innovation, it houses five movable stages. At the opposite end of the spectrum, the nearby **Marché d'Aligre (4)** *(Pl. d'Aligre, 12th)*, a frolicking food market with second-hand antique stalls, embodies the working-class character of the area.

Arts & Entertainment:

In addition to its opera season, **Opéra Bastille (3)** *(see also above)* offers free lunchtime events ("Casse-Croûte à l'Opéra") every Thursday. The **Pavillon de l'Arsenal (5)** *(21 bd. Morland, 4th, 01-42.76.33.97, www.pavillon-arsenal.com)*, in an old 19th-century iron and glass ware-house, covers the urban development and architectural history of Paris through photos, descriptions, and scale models; in individual video booths you can watch any of 120 films about Paris's architects and their work, or watch a film about the city in the video lounge. You can also catch one of the temporary exhibits of big names in architecture.

Check out exhibits of contemporary artists at galleries in **Rue de Charonne**, **Rue de Lappe**, and **Rue Keller**.

PLACES TO EAT & DRINK
Where to Eat:

At **Le Train Bleu (6)** (€€-€€€) *(Place Louis Armand, 12th, 01-43.43.09.06, www.le-train-bleu.com)* ambience is everything: the murals and frescoed ceilings of this fabulous belle-époque brasserie will transport you. It's okay to have just a glass of champagne and stare at the walls. The Bastille area is surrounded by good, affordable bistros, once the staple of working-class life and now destinations for trendy aficionados and locals alike. **Le Viaduc Café (7)** (€€) *(43 ave. Daumesnil, 12th, 01-44.74.70.70, www.viaduc-café.fr)*, under the reno-

vated railroad viaduct, is pretty and noisy with lots of pavement tables; best for its Sunday jazz brunch. Put together fabulous Belle Époque décor, creative cuisine, and a rising neighborhood chic factor, and you get supermodels and other celebs swarming to **Le Square Trousseau (8)** (€€) *(1 rue Antoine Vollon, 12th, 01-43.43.06.00)*. **Le China Club (9)** (€€) *(50 rue Charenton, 12th, 01-43.43.82.02, www.chinaclub.cc)* is a happening scene with a mix of grand themes, from Art Deco to colonial cool to speakeasy chic; the Chinese food may not be the best, but the ambience makes up for it. The stylishness of **Ramulaud (10)** (€€) *(269 rue Faubourg-St-Antoine, 11th, 01-43.72.23.29)* has contributed to its growing popularity; pols and activists are among the clientele. Three restaurants stand out in **Rue Paul-Bert** for consistently good food, excellent wine, and great atmosphere: **Le Temps au Temps (11)** (€€) *(13 rue Paul-Bert, 11th, 01-43.79.63.40)*, small and cozy with good contemporary cuisine; **L'Ecailler du Bistrot (12)** (€€) *(20-22 rue Paul-Bert, 11th, 01-43.72.76.77)*, maybe the best fish and seafood bistro in Paris, famous for its oysters; and **Bistrot Paul Bert (13)** (€€-€€€) *(18 rue Paul-Bert, 11th, 01-43.72.24.01)*, old-fashioned and simple, with generous portions and an owner who'll talk about wine at the drop of a hat. Recalling the 1930s, **Le Vieux Chêne (14)** (€€-€€€) *(7 rue Dahomey, 11th, 01-43.71.67.69)* is a handsome bistro that's just the right fit for your antique-crawling expedition. **Pause Café (15)** *(41 rue de Charonne, 11th, 01-48.06.80.33)* is welcoming with lots of outdoor seating; try the tomato and cucumber soup, and chicken sautéed in coconut milk and basil. Those trendsetters and rockers love the couscous at **Le Souk (16)** (€€) *(1 rue Keller, 11th, 01-49.29.05.08)*; you might admire the covered bazaar ambience of this Moroccan restaurant. Though there's no choice on the menu, **Au C'Amelot (17)** (€€) *(50 rue Amelot, 11th, 01-43.55.54.04)* serves sophisticated bistro cuisine at budget prices. **Le Villaret (39)** (€€) *(13 rue Ternaux, 11th, 01-43.57.89.69)* is a fabulous neighborhood bistro with creative renditions of classic French cuisine; the crowds you're likely to find there will have a mix of wine

connoisseurs, neighborhood old hats, and a sprinkling of hipsters.

Bars & Nightlife:

The oldest *musette* dance hall in Paris, **Le Balajo (18)** *(9 rue de Lappe, 11th, 01-47.00.07.87)* has an old-fashioned atmosphere that appeals, with 1950s, 1960s, 1970s music, salsa, and disco on varying nights. **Rue de Charonne** is full of cafés and wine bars. The relaxed **Le Café du Passage (19)** *(12 Rue de Charonne, 11th, 01-49. 29.97.64)* offers more than 300 wines of great vintages. **Le China Club (9)** *(see also page 90)* has a great bar on the first floor and weekend jazz concerts in the basement. Further to the east, **La Muse Vin (20)** *(101 rue de Charonne, 11th, 01-40.09.93.05)* is a "natural" wine bar (organic wine made without industrial additives), with wines mostly unknown in the U.S. (beware the heavy cigarette smoke). At the bar **LeWax (21)** *(15 rue Daval, 11th, 01-40.21.16.16)* the décor is a throwback to the psychedelic 1960s. Of the plentiful cool cafés around the Bastille, **Café de l'Industrie (22)** *(16 rue St-Sabin,*

11th, 01-47.00.13.53, www.cafede lindustrie.com), a local haunt, is one of the cheeriest and friendliest. The wine bar **Le Vin de Zinc (42)** *(25 rue Oberkampf, 11th, 01-48.06.28.23)* offers all the favorite reds and whites, mostly without sulphates (to prevent those pesky headaches); they also serve large portions of hearty foods, like steak and fries.

WHERE TO SHOP

Renovated and glassed in, the arcades of an old railway viaduct house the Viaduc des Arts (23) *(1-129 ave. Daumesnil, 12th, www.viaduc-des-arts.com)*, with its craft shops, galleries, exhibition spaces, and open *ateliers* where artisans weave and hammer, stitch and iron. Salient among them: **Créations Chérif** *(No. 13)*, with sofas and chairs; **Maison Fey** *(No. 15)* for embossed books, frames, and furnishings; **VIA** *(Valorisation de l'Innovation dans l'Ameublement, Nos. 29-33)*, exhibiting textiles, furniture, and home accessories; **Vertical** *(No. 63)*, with sculptural wood and vegetation; and **Cyrille Varet** *(No. 67)*, featuring wild sculpted steel furniture, in vibrant upholstery. There are real "finds" among the secondhand merchandise at the **Marché d'Aligre (4)** *(see also page 89)*. Isabel Marant (24) *(16 rue de Charonne, 11th, 01-49.29.71.55)* designs feminine clothing in silks, cashmere, and other fine fabrics. In **Rue Keller**, the seductive mohair creations of Gaëlle Barré (25) *(17 rue Keller, 11th, 01-43.14.63.02)* will turn your head. A few doors away, Anne Willi (26) *(13 rue Keller, 11th, 01-48.06.74.06)* designs are elegant and versatile. With three floors of vintage delight at Come On Eileen (27) *(16-18 rue des Taillandiers, 11th, 01-43.38.12.11)*, pieces range from funky cowboy duds to Hermès scarves.

WHERE TO STAY

Hotels are less expensive in this working-class area. Rooms are plain, spare, but sizable at **Hôtel Lyon-Mulhouse (28)** (€) *(8 bd. Beaumarchais, 11th, 01-47.00.91.50, www.1-hotel-paris.com)* and some have lovely views. Functional rooms with A/C and access to the galleries, cafés, and boutiques of the area make Daval Hôtel (29) (€) *(21 rue Daval, 11th, 01-47.00.51.23)* a good budget choice. A hop away from the Opéra Bastille, Hôtel le Pavillon Bastille (30) (€€) *(65 rue de Lyon, 12th, 01-43.43.65.65)*, with its blue and yellow color scheme and young, friendly staff, is bright and cheery; no A/C makes traffic noise on street-side rooms problematic. An alternative is a studio apartment at the Centre Parisien de Zen (31) (€) (cheap weekly rates) *(35 rue de Lyon, 12th, 01-44.87.08.13, www.maisonzen. com)*: sunny, whitewashed units with Ikea furnishings surround a tree-lined cobblestone courtyard. Close to the Place de la République, Hôtel Notre-Dame (46) (€) *(51 rue de Malte, 11th, 01-47.00.78.76, www.hotel-notredame.com)* offers minimal comfort but is clean; some rooms have no bathrooms. Hôtel Plessis (47) (€) *(25 rue du Grand Prieuré, 11th, 01-47.00.13.38)* also provides clean, adequate rooms, though a few share bathrooms. A very cheap sleep will rescue the budget weary at Hôtel de Nevers (48) (€) *(53 rue de Malte, 11th, 01-47.00.56.18, www.hoteldenevers.com)*; it's clean but furnishings consist basically of a bed only, and bathrooms are shared.

CANAL ST-MARTIN

③ ⑤ ⑧ ⑨ ⑪ *to République;*
⑤ *to Jacques Bonsergent;* **②** *to Colonel Fabien;*
⑦ *to Château Landon or Louis Blanc;*
② ⑤ ⑦ᵇⁱˢ *to Jaurès;* **② ⑤ ⑦** *to Stalingrad*

● SNAPSHOT ●

With Marais rents soaring, emerging designers, artists, and media start-ups are moving northward to the increasingly hip and bohemian Canal St-Martin. Overwhelmingly for the young (20- and 30-some-things), the area is fast becoming the "in" place. Its less frenetic pace gives it a village atmosphere with urban sophistication. The three-mile canal, a Seine shortcut, is fascinating to observe as boats maneuver adroitly through locks and under bridges.

PLACES TO SEE
Landmarks:

From the **Place de la République** all the way up to the end of the canal at **Bassin de la Villette**, the working-class underpinnings of the Canal St-

Martin area are evident. The houses, taverns, cafés, ware-houses, and factories all reveal aspects of that 19th-century world. In the **Rue du Faubourg-du-Temple (32)** *(starting at Place de la République, 10th)*, a busy street full of ethnic shops and restaurants, details on some buildings and storefronts testify to the care taken in embellishing this working-class neighborhood. However, even the 17th-century **St-Louis Hospital (33)** *(Rue Bichat, 10th)*, beautiful though it is, has none of the luxurious ornamentation of the more aristocratic Right Bank districts bordering the river. The best way to see the area is to take a **boat trip** up the canal, passing under romantic footbridges and through its nine locks: you board a Canauxrama boat at **Port de l'Arsenal (34)** *(opposite 50 bd. de la Bastille, 12th, 01-42.39.15.00 for a three-hour ride, See Bastille neighborhood on map)*. Alternatively, walking along the **Quai de Valmy** or **Quai de Jemmapes** is a relaxed way of absorbing young, cutting-edge Paris and the making of chic.

PLACES TO EAT & DRINK
Where to Eat:

With the Canal St-Martin attracting converts, "funk" is in and **Chez Prune (35) (€€)** *(36 rue Beaurepaire, 10th, 01-42.41.30.47)* has become a prime example of a trendy café-bar. Eclectic and unpretentious, its strongest appeal is the view over the canal on the **Quai de Valmy**. Another café popular in this youthful neighborhood is **La Marine (36) (€€)** *(55 bis, quai de Valmy, 10th, 01-42.39.69.81)*. Brazilian home-style food at **Favela Chic (37) (€€)** *(18 rue du Faubourg-du-Temple, 11th, 01-40.21.38.14, www.favelachic.com)* mixed with irresistible music will have you dancing between courses. Romantic **Hôtel du Nord (38) (€)** *(102 quai de Jemmapes, 10th, 01-40.40.78.78)*, where the 1938 film of the same

LATIN QUARTER
ÎLE DE LA CITÉ
ÎLE ST-LOUIS

Places to See:

1. Place St-Michel
2. Shakespeare & Co.
3. St-Julien-le-Pauvre
4. St-Séverin
5. National Museum of the Middle Ages (Cluny Museum)
6. Sorbonne
7. Collège de France
8. Panthéon
9. Place de la Contrescarpe
10. Rue Mouffetard
11. Paris Mosque
12. Jardin des Plantes
13. National Museum of Natural History
14. Arènes de Lutèce
15. Institute of the Arab World
57. Square du Vert-Galant
58. Place Dauphine
59. Palais de Justice
60. Sainte-Chapelle
61. Conciergerie
62. Flower and Bird Market
63. Crypte Archéologique
64. Notre-Dame
65. Museum of Notre-Dame de Paris
67. Hôtel Chernizot
68. Hôtel Lambert
69. St-Louis

Places to Eat & Drink:

16. La Fourmi Ailée
17. Le Reminet
18. L'Atelier Maître Albert
19. Le Pré Verre
20. Brasserie Balzar
21. Chantairelle
22. Le Berthoud
23. Les Fontaines
24. Perraudin
25. Café de la Nouvelle Mairie
26. Les Quatre et Une Saveurs
27. L'Assiette aux Fromages
28. Mouff' Tartes
29. Le Jardin des Pâtes
30. La Petite Légume
31. Au Moulin à Vent "Chez Henri"
32. La Tour d'Argent
33. La Rôtisserie de Beaujolais
34. Inagiku

Where to Shop:

Where to Stay:

LATIN QUARTER

4 to St-Michel;
10 to Cluny-La Sorbonne or Maubert-Mutualité;
7 to Censier-Daubentonn or Place Monge;
7 **10** to Jussieu; **10** to Cardinal Lemoine

• SNAPSHOT •

The Latin Quarter is the student district where Paris's first university, the Sorbonne, was founded in 1253. At the time, Latin was the language of scholars; thus the area acquired its name. Still buzzing with students and full of different ethnic influences, the Latin Quarter, though commercial and touristy, remains bohemian, vibrant, and full of young people. Although the echoes of the famous 1968 student/worker strike have long faded, the inexpensive shops, ethnic boutiques, avant-garde theatres, and cinemas remain, as do vestiges of much earlier times. Around Boulevard St-Michel, the main street, is a labyrinth of cobblestoned passages, and the Rue St-Jacques, an old Roman road, is the precursor of all Parisian streets. The Latin Quarter and its eastern flank, Jussieu, are full of interesting museums, from the magnificent medieval Cluny Museum to the breathtaking Institute of the Arab World with its modern architectural design based on age-old Islamic

motifs. Even the Jardin des Plantes, one of Paris's great parks, includes a zoo, botanical school, and the natural history museum and study center, in keeping with the Latin Quarter's centuries-old dedication to culture and learning.

PLACES TO SEE
Landmarks:
At the north end of the busy Boulevard St-Michel, or "Boul'Mich," its nickname, is the **Place St-Michel (1)**, with its ornately sculpted fountain. The site of Paris Commune uprisings in 1871 and student unrest in May 1968, it is now a common meeting point for students. The square borders the river, facing the Pont St-Michel bridge. A stroll along these quays of the Seine is a must: they're filled with the famous bookstalls, the **bouquinistes**. Around the corner from Place St-Michel, along the quay, is **Shakespeare & Co. (2)** *(37 rue de la Bûcherie, 5th, 01-43.26.96.50, www.shakespeareco.org, open 12-12)*, the chaotic but cozy anglophone bookstore famous for the stream of literati who've flowed through its doors. Nearby, the church of **St-Julien-le-Pauvre (3)** *(1 rue St-Julien-le-Pauvre, 5th, 01-43.29.  09.09)*, now Greek Orthodox, is one of the oldest in Paris. A short, narrow street in this area, the **Rue Galande**, is synonymous with notorious taverns. A few cobbled streets away, the flamboyant Gothic church **St-Séverin (4)** *(1 rue des Prêtres-St-Séverin, 5th, 01-42.34. 93.50)* flaunts its beauty with spires, balustrades, and gargoyles.

Perhaps the jewel of the Latin Quarter is the **National Museum of the Middle Ages (5)** *(6 pl. Paul-Painlevé, 5th, 01-53.73.78.00, www.musee-moyenage.fr)*, often referred to by its previous name, the Cluny Museum. A unique combination of Gallo-Roman ruins, baths dating from 200 AD, and a medieval mansion built by the Abbot of Cluny in 1500, the museum affords the traveler a trip into history, in both its ambience and its collection.

The **Sorbonne (6)** *(47 rue des Écoles, 5th, 01-40.46.22.11)*, seat of the 13 autonomous University of Paris branches and a world-famous institution of learning, has produced some of the most important intellectuals in history. In the main courtyard, the **Chapel of the Sorbonne** is a monument to Richelieu. Across the street is the research institute **Collège de France (7)** *(11 place Marcelin-Berthelot, 5th, 01-44.27.12.11)*, founded in 1530.

A few streets south is the **Panthéon (8)** *(Place du Panthéon, 5th, 01-44.32.18.00)*, originally designed to be an 18th-century neoclassical church, which was built by Louis XV. After surviving a terrible illness, he wanted to give thanks, so he dedicated the building to the patron saint of Paris, Sainte Geneviève; murals telling her story line its interior walls. After the French Revolution, it was turned into a pantheon, the crypt of great figures of France: Voltaire, Jean-Jacques Rousseau,

Émile Zola, Victor Hugo, Pierre and Marie Curie, Jean Moulin, and Jean Monnet, father of the European Community, are entombed here.

Other prominent figures have trod the pavement of **Place de la Contrescarpe (9)** (*5th*). This is where the 16th-century group of writers known as *La Pléiade* used to meet. Ernest Hemingway lived in **39 rue Descartes** when he was an unknown writer, then later with his wife Hadley at **74 rue du Cardinal-Lemoine.**

Today's Parisians teem in the **Rue Mouffetard (10)** (*5th*). It's one of the city's oldest thoroughfares, dating from Roman times. You can still see ancient painted signs on some shops. This pedestrian street is famous today for its open-air markets, especially in **Place Maubert**, **Place Monge**, and the adjacent **Rue Daubenton**, home to an upbeat African market. Follow Rue Daubenton eastward and you'll arrive at the **Paris Mosque (11)** (*2 bis, pl. du puits de l'Ermite, 5th, 01-45.35.97.33, www.mosquee-de-paris.net*). Built in Hispano-Moorish style, the spiritual structure is a splendid creation incorporating decorative tiles, intricately carved lace-like wood screens, and magnificent carpets. The interior patio garden was modeled on the Alhambra in Granada. Its café serves traditional mint tea and delicious pastries. An authentic hammam is open on alternate days to men and women.

Across from the mosque, the **Jardin des Plantes (12)** (*57 rue Cuvier, 5th*), Paris's botanical garden, boasts ancient trees and remarkable displays of wild and herbaceous plants. It also features a zoo, a botanical school, and the

National Museum of Natural History (13) *(2 rue Buffon, 5th, 01-40.79.36.00, www.mnhn.fr)*. To the northwest, the **Arènes de Lutèce (14)** *(Rue de Navarre, 5th)*, the remains of a Gallo-Roman arena (Romans named Paris "Lutetia"), was probably used for theatrical performances and gladiator fights, a combined use particular to Gaul. Seating 15,000, it was arranged in 35 tiers. Winding northward, you arrive at the **Institute of the Arab World (15)** *(1 rue des Fossées-St-Bernard, 5th, 01-40.51.38.38, www.imarabe.org)*, designed by French architect Jean Nouvel. A breathtaking building that encapsulates the spirit and motifs of traditional Arab architecture using modern materials, this cultural institute and museum was founded in 1980 by France and 20 Arab nations and dedicated to nurturing cultural understanding and cooperation between the Islamic world and the West. The southern façade comprises 1,600 high-tech metal screens; modeled on Moorish screens of carved wood, they filter the sunlight entering the building.

Arts & Entertainment:

For chamber and religious music concerts, **St-Julien-le-Pauvre (3)** *(see also page 102)* is the perfect venue. English-language bookstore **Shakespeare & Co. (2)** *(see also page 102)* hosts poetry readings. The cultural wealth of the Latin Quarter lies in its museums. Besides a superb collection of illuminated manuscripts, sculptures, ceramics, woodcarvings, precious metals, and

Gallo-Roman ruins, the **National Museum of the Middle Ages (5)** (also known as Cluny Museum) *(see also page 103)* is home to the famous **Lady with the Unicorn**, a series of six exquisite 15th-century tapestries, the **Gallery of the Kings**, 21 stone heads of the Kings of Judah (13th century), two **Books of Hours** (15th century), and the **Golden Rose of Basel**, a rose sculpted in gold for the Avignon Pope John XXII (14th century). Columns, a pediment relief, and a grandiose dome lend majesty to the façade of the **Panthéon (8)** *(see also page 103)*. Inside, frescoes, statues, and decorative archways are appropriate monuments in this shrine to great personages of French history. On several floors of the magnificent **Institute of the Arab World (15)** *(see also page 105)*, Islamic works of art span the 9th to 19th centuries. The lower level displays art works from the Arab world since 1950: photography, graphic arts, painting, sculpture, and calligraphy. The **National Museum of Natural History (13)** *(see also page 105)* fascinates with its exhibits of humans and animals as well as its mineralogical and gemstone displays. It's famous for its Grand Hall of Evolution.

PLACES TO EAT & DRINK
Where to Eat:

For a long, cozy lunch, **La Fourmi Ailée (16)** (€) *(8 rue du Fouarre, 5th, 01-43.29.40.99)* specializes in tarts; the service is slow but the library-den ambience is charming. **Le Reminet (17)** (€€) *(3 rue des Grands-Degrés, 5th, 01-44.07.04.24)* was a well-kept secret, but the word is out: the food's memorable; the service delightful. Country flair, Latin Quarter buzz, and a view of Notre-Dame add atmosphere to the classic fare at **L'Atelier Maître Albert (18)** (€€) *(1 rue Maître-Albert, 5th, 01-46.33.13.78)*. Just north of the Sorbonne, **Le Pré Verre (19)** (€€) *(8 rue Thénard, 5th, 01-43.54.59.47)*, one of the newest bistros, charming and casual, whips up inventive dishes with exotic spices, appropriate for the background jazz music. Rub elbows with Left Bank pundits at **Brasserie Balzar (20)** (€€) *(49 rue des Ecoles, 5th, 01-43.54.13.67)*; it hasn't changed much since Sartre and Camus used to drop in, sawdust on the floor and all. **Chantairelle (21)** (€€-€€€) *(17 rue de Laplace, 5th, 01-46.33.18.59, www.chantairelle.com)*, with its hearty food and rustic décor, is so authentic you might think you were in the Auvergne. Romance mixes with healthy dishes at **Le Berthoud (22)** (€€) *(1 rue Valette, 5th, 01-43.54.38.81)*.

Restaurants around the Panthéon aren't fussy. Though **Les Fontaines (23)** (€€) *(9 rue Soufflot, 5th, 01-43.26.42.80)* looks shabby, it's a favorite of

locals, lowly and elite alike. For home-style French classics, **Perraudin (24)** (€€) *(157 rue St-Jacques, 5th, 01-46.33.15.75)* is the real thing; so typically 1900s, down to the Turkish toilet! **Café de la Nouvelle Mairie (25)** (€-€€) *(19-21 rue des Fossés-St-Jacques, 5th, 01-44.07.04. 41)* is the perfect café: friendly, relaxing, with a lovely terrace.

Toward **Rue Mouffetard (10)**, **Les Quatre et Une Saveurs (26)** (€) *(72 rue du Cardinal-Lemoine, 5th, 01-43.26.88.80)* serves delicious organic vegetarian dishes. Beware the tourist traps along **Rue Mouffetard (10)**. However, rest assured that **L'Assiette aux Fromages (27)** (€-€€) *(27 rue Mouffetard, 5th, 01-45.35.14.21)* isn't

one of them. It's all things cheese—fondue, quiches, tarts, raclette—along with great bread and salads. A good cheap eat is **Mouff' Tartes (28)** (€) *(53 rue Mouffetard, 5th, 01-43.37.21.89)*, with great quiches and yummy chocolate desserts.

Across from the Jardin des Plantes, the organic pasta at **Le Jardin des Pâtes (29)** (€) *(4 rue Lacépède, 5th, 01-43.31.50.71)* is delicious: try the chestnut (*châtaigne*) pasta with duck fillet, mushrooms, and cream. Try bargain vegetarian fare at **La Petite Légume (30)** (€) *(36 rue des Boulangers, 5th, 01-40.46.06.85)*. On the other end of the spectrum, **Au Moulin à Vent "Chez Henri" (31)** (€€-€€€) *(20 rue des Fossés-St-Bernard, 5th, 01-43.54.99.37)* is known for great steaks.

Very expensive, very entrancing, and one of Paris's most fabled restaurants, **La Tour d'Argent (32)** (€€€) *(17 quai de la Tournelle, 5th, 01-43.54.23.31, www.latourdargent.com)* is high-class with a fabulous view of Notre-Dame. Its modestly-priced neighbor, **La Rôtisserie de Beaujolais (33)** (€€) *(19 quai de la Tournelle, 5th, 01-43.54.17.47)* has the same view and feeds bustling crowds with less fancy, but tasty, dependable classics. Try fresh seafood, sizzling in front of you on the teppanyaki grill, at **Inagiku (34)** (€€€) *(14 rue de Pontoise, 5th, 01-43.54.70.07).*

Bars & Nightlife:

Medieval cellars around St-Michel have turned into jazz clubs: **Caveau de la Huchette (35)** *(5 rue de la Huchette, 5th, 01-43.26.65.05)* and **Caveau des Oubliettes (36)** *(25 rue Galande, 5th, 01-46.34.23.09)* are on the tourist circuit, but they offer good acts. Student nightlife buzzes around **Place de la Contrescarpe (9)** *(see also page 104),*

full of tiny bars and cafés. Check out **Café Egyptien (37)** *(112 rue Mouffetard, 5th, 01-43.31.11.35)* for Arab music, mint tea, and a midnight nosh. On Sunday evenings from June to October the **Square Tino Rossi (38)** *(5th)* on the banks of the Seine by the Jardin des Plantes fills with hip-shaking rhythm lovers dancing their feet off—rumba, mambo, tango, samba, you name it, they'll swing.

WHERE TO SHOP

The Latin Quarter is full of small shops, mostly catering to students' needs and wallets. Stroll by the **bouquinistes**, the stalls along the quays of the Seine: you'll find new and old books (even first editions), prints, maps, and postcards. **Shakespeare & Co. (2)** *(see also page 102)* is the mecca for English-language book lovers. Shop at Librairie Gibert Joseph (39) *(26, 30, 32, 34 bd. St-Michel, 5th, 01-44.41.88.88)* for new and used books, CDs, and notebooks. Jeanne et Jérémy (40) *(4 rue Frédéric-Sauton,*

5th, 01-46.33.54.54) is teddy bear heaven; these are designed by artists. The treasure trove of toys at La Tortue Electrique (41) *(7 rue Frédéric-Sauton, 5th, 01-43.29.37.08)* will send you back to your childhood, while the divinely scented candles at Diptyque (42) *(34 bd. St-Germain, 5th, 01-43.26.45.27)* will transport you back to France when they're burning in your home long after your trip.

Gourmet cookbooks, old and new, abound at Librairie Gourmande (43) *(4 rue Dante, 5th, 01-43.54.37.27, www.librairie-gourmande.fr)*; they include French, American, and English editions. Les Papilles (44) *(30 rue Gay-Lussac, 5th, 01-43.25.20.79)* stocks regional French gourmet foods. It is also a restaurant, and a gourmet-lover's delight. Products from Brittany—pea coats, sweaters, striped Breton T-shirts, pottery—are the real thing at Les Artisans du Rêve: Breiz Noway (45) *(33 rue Gay-Lussac, 5th, 01-43.29.47.82)*. For shopping or gawking, the open-air markets on **Rue Mouffetard (10)** *(see also page 104)* and the African market on **Rue Daubenton** afford an authentic Parisian experience. La Tuile à Loup (46) *(35 rue Daubenton, 5th, 01-47.07.28. 90)* sells regional French table and housewares. Nearby Marché Monge (47) *(Place Monge, 5th; Wed., Fri., Sun., 8 AM-2 PM)*, less touristy, is full of feisty produce hawkers.

Old World door handles and other lovely fixtures can be found at the hardware store La Quincaillerie (48) *(3 bd. St-Germain, 5th, 01-46.33.66.71).* Comptoirs Tour d'Argent Art de la Table (49) *(2 rue du Cardinal-Lemoine, 5th, 01-46.33.45.58)*, the famous restaurant's shop, sells fine china, crystal, and silverware.

WHERE TO STAY

The rooms at **Hôtel Agora St-Germain (50)** (€-€€) *(42 rue des Bernardins, 5th, 01-46.34.13.00, www. AgoraSaintGermain.com)* have space, silk wallpaper, marble-tiled bathrooms, and A/C (not a given in non-luxury hotels). Located across a tree-filled square, **Hôtel Résidence Henri IV (51)** (€€) *(50 rue des Bernardins, 5th, 01-44.41.31.81, www.residencehenri4.com)* is quiet and comfortable; kitchenettes and lovely two-room suites are available.

Facing the Sorbonne, **Grand Hôtel St-Michel (52)** (€€) *(19 rue Cujas, 5th, 01-46.33.33.02, www. grand-hotel-st-michel.com)* has a sophisticated look, with spacious rooms, A/C, and hand-painted

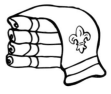

furniture. An elegant converted 18th-century town-house, the Hôtel du Panthéon (53) (€€) *(19 pl. du Panthéon, 5th, 01-43.54.32.95, www.hoteldupantheon. com)*, with its atrium garden and view of the Panthéon, is tastefully appointed with antique furniture, coordinated fabrics, and framed artwork in high-ceilinged rooms.

Familia Hôtel (54) (€) *(11 rue des Écoles, 5th, 01-43.54. 55.27, www.hotel-paris-familia.com)* is a great deal; exposed stone walls or painted murals coordinate with tapestry wall-hangings. Another bargain is the Hôtel des Grandes Écoles (55) (€) *(75 rue du Cardinal-Lemoine, 5th, 01-43.26.79.23, www.hotel-grandes-ecoles.com)*: the terrace overlooks a garden, which will transport you to a peaceful French countryside setting after a long day of city sightseeing.

Hôtel Relais Saint-Jacques (56) (€€-€€€) *(3 rue de l'Abbé-de-l'Épée, 5th, 01-53.73.26.00, toll-free in U.S. 800-44-UTELL, www.relais-saint-jacques.com)* is a boutique hotel inspired by the Loire Valley's châteaux; traditional décor and modern amenities create a luxurious experience.

ÎLE DE LA CITÉ

4 *to Cité or St-Michel;* **1 4 7 14** *to Châtelet*

• SNAPSHOT •

Île de la Cité is where Paris began: around 250 BCE a tribe of Celtic Gauls, river traders called the Parisii, settled on the island. With the river encircling it like a moat, it was easily defendable. Île de la Cité became the seat of power and the site of a royal palace (now the law courts). Monumental buildings arose: Notre-Dame Cathedral, Sainte-Chapelle, and the Conciergerie. These historical buildings lend majesty to the island and magnificence to the riverfront. Amid the enormity of its power and beauty, the island still contains pockets of smaller-scale charm.

PLACES TO SEE
Landmarks:

The western tip of the island, the tree-lined triangle of the **Square du Vert-Galant (57)** *(1st)*, named after the amorous King Henri IV, is one of the most beautiful areas of Paris. The Seine stretches out on either side; beyond the river, Paris sprawls at your feet. **Pont Neuf** ("New Bridge"), the oldest bridge in Paris, connects the island to the rest of the city. To the east is **Place Dauphine (58)** *(1st)*, another haven of charm and calm. The **Palais de Justice (59)** *(4 bd. du Palais, 1st, 01-44.32.50.00)*, now the law courts, was for centuries the royal palace, until the king moved to the Marais in the 14th century. During the French Revolution, the site became a tribunal. Nestled among the courts, **Sainte-Chapelle (60)** *(4 bd. du Palais, 1st, 01-53.73.78.50)* is among Europe's greatest architectural masterpieces. Famous for its 15 magnificent stained-glass windows depicting more than 1,000 religious scenes, the chapel is characterized by lofty vaulted ceilings. Louis IX built the chapel in 1248 to house Christian relics, including what was purported to be Christ's crown of thorns.

To the north is the **Conciergerie (61)** *(1 quai de l'Horloge, 1st, 01-53.40.60.97)*, the prison made infamous during the Revolution. Marie Antoinette was jailed there until her execution; so were Charlotte Corday, who stabbed Revolutionary leader Marat; and Revolutionary judges Danton and Robespierre. East of the Conciergerie, the famous **Flower and Bird Market (62)** *(Pl. Louis-Lépine, 4th)* adds a splash of life and color to an area of daunting administrative buildings. Gallo-Roman ruins and vestiges of 2,000-year-old houses are on view in the **Crypte Archéologique (63)** *(Pl. du Parvis-Notre-Dame, 4th, 01-55.42.50.10)*. It is located on the main square of one of Paris's most famous structures, the Gothic cathedral of

 **Notre-Dame (64)** *(Pl. du Parvis-Notre-Dame, 4th, 01-42.34. 56.10)*. Noted for its flying buttresses, gargoyles (you can climb up 387 steps in the North Tower to the **Galerie des Chimères** to view these famous carved creatures), and two rose windows of stained glass, the cathedral is

a marvel inside and out. Masterpieces of statuary cover the three main doors. Inside, statues, reliefs, paintings, and carved woodwork add to the grandeur. Kings and emperors were crowned beneath these lofty vaults.

Arts & Entertainment:

Notre-Dame (64), Sainte-Chapelle (60), the Conciergerie (61), and the Crypte Archéologique (63) are among Paris's most fascinating and oldest treasures. To get an even closer look at historical treasures, visit the Museum of Notre-Dame de Paris (65) *(10 rue du Cloître-Notre-Dame, 4th, 01-43.25.42.92)*, which contains documents, relics, objects, and engravings covering the history of Notre-Dame.

PLACES TO EAT & DRINK
Where to Eat:

Restaurants aren't abundant in this area, so you might be better off eating on Île St-Louis. However, **Le Vieux Bistro (66) (€€)** *(14 rue du Cloître-Notre-Dame, 4th, 01-43.54.18.95)*, a classic French bistro, serves great Lyonnais cuisine.

WHERE TO SHOP

The shopping here is basically limited to souvenirs and postcards. Stick to sightseeing and leave shopping for your spin around St-Germain.

WHERE TO STAY

There's not much in the way of lodging in this administrative district. Try Île St-Louis or other nearby areas (Marais, Latin Quarter, and St-Germain).

ÎLE ST-LOUIS

7 *to Pont Marie;* **10** *to Cardinal Lemoine*

• SNAPSHOT •

One of the most beautiful areas of Paris, the Île St-Louis is a haven of serenity and elegance between the bustle and noise of the Left and Right Banks.

Splendid 17th-century residences line calm streets, and along the romantic quays of the river the views are fabulous. It's a favorite residential area of artists and heiresses—and home to members of the Rothschild family. This is the perfect place to find a moment of repose after days of sightseeing.

PLACES TO SEE
Landmarks:

Stroll the periphery of the island: you'll find not only marvelous views of the city, but also lovely corners, beautiful residences, exquisite wrought-iron balconies, graceful doorways, and superb statuary. Check out the gargoyles that hold up the balcony at **Hôtel Chernizot (67)** *(51 rue St-Louis-en-l'Ile, 4th)* and don't miss **Hôtel Lambert (68)** *(Rue St-Louis-en-l'Ile at Quai d'Anjou, 4th)*, a famous aristocratic 17th-century townhouse. The carved doors of the island church, **St-Louis (69)** *(corner of Rue St-Louis-en-l'Ile and Rue Poulletier, 4th)*, are splendid; its clock and tower are also beautiful.

PLACES TO EAT & DRINK
Where to Eat:

With a spectacular view of Notre-Dame and the river, **Le Flore en l'Ile (70)** (€€) *(42 quai d'Orléans, 4th, 01-43.29.88.27)* is fabulous for breakfast, tea, desserts; less so for meals. Enjoy a great Alsatian meal at **Brasserie de l'Ile St-Louis (71)** (€€) *(55 quai de Bourbon, 4th, 01-43.54.02.59)*, a favorite of the island's cognoscenti. **Rue St-Louis-en-l'Ile** is the main drag with several appetizing eateries. For a light meal of quiche, salad, *crêpe*, and the like, **Au Lys d'Argent (72)** (€) *(90 rue St-Louis-en-l'Ile, 4th, 01-46.33.65.13)* satisfies many tastes and serves brunch daily. The chef at **Mon Vieil Ami (73)** (€€) *(69 rue St-Louis-en-l'Ile, 4th, 01-40.46.01.35)* creates imaginative, masterful Alsatian concoctions, lighter than the traditional fare, in a beautiful modern interior. For ethnic variety, **La Castafiore (74)** (€-€€) *(51 rue St-Louis-en-l'Ile, 4th, 01-43.54.78.62)* serves wonderful Italian dishes; tiny and sometimes cramped, it's romantically cozy outside rush hours. Robust country classics have local families returning to **Gourmet de l'Isle (75)** (€-€€) *(42 rue St-Louis-en-l'Ile, 4th, 01-43.26.79.27)*. Farm food and partying go hand-in-hand at **Nos Ancêtres les Gaulois (76)** (€€) *(39 rue St-Louis-en-l'Ile, 4th, 01-46.33.66.07)*, an all-you-can-eat country inn with long trestle tables. A visit to Paris isn't complete without a stop at the famous ice cream

parlor **Berthillon (77) (€)** *(31 rue St-Louis-en-l'Ile, 4th, 01-43.54.31.61)*: all Parisians know it's the best around. Pastries, chocolates, pure fruit lollipops—**La Charlotte de l'Ile (78) (€)** *(24 rue St-Louis-en-l'Ile, 4th, 01-43.54.25.83, www.la-charlotte.fr)* is a sweet lover's delight. The sign in the window says: "Here we sell happiness."

WHERE TO SHOP

Besides restaurants, **Rue St-Louis-en-l'Ile** is also the main shopping street. Chocolate pyramids and spicy fillings are just some of the delicacies at Cacao et Chocolat (79) *(63 rue St-Louis-en-l'Ile, 4th, 01-46.33.33.33).* L'Epicerie (80) *(51 rue St-Louis-en-l'Ile, 4th, 01-43.25.20.14)* is a great gourmet food gift shop—pick up delicious souvenirs for the folks back home. The funny neckties and suspenders you may have seen at the Pompidou Center are made and sold at Pylones (81) *(57 rue St-Louis-en-l'Ile, 4th, 01-46.34.05.02).* Stop in Yamina (82) *(56 rue St-Louis-en-l'Ile, 4th, 01-43.29.33.93)* for hand-painted scarves and women's clothing. Beads galore, cords, and clasps—make your own jewelry masterpieces at Le Grain de Sable (83) *(79 rue St-Louis-en-l'Ile, 4th, 01-46.33.67.27)* or buy the salespeople's creations.

WHERE TO STAY

The hotels on **Rue St-Louis-en-l'Ile** reflect the romantic charm of the island and its calm, dignified pace. The intimate atmosphere of Hôtel Saint-Louis (84) (€€) *(75 rue St-Louis-en-l'Ile, 4th, 01-46.34.04.80, www.hotel saintlouis.com)*—with exposed wood beams, tapestry fabrics, antiques, and flowers—makes up for the small

ST-GERMAIN
RUE DU BAC
MONTPARNASSE

Places to See:

Places to Eat & Drink:

Where to Stay:

④ *to St-Germain-des-Prés, St-Sulpice,*
   St-Michel, or St-Placide;
⑩ *to Mabillon;* ④ ⑩ *to Odéon;*
⑫ *to Rennes or Notre-Dame-des-Champs;*

• SNAPSHOT •

St-Germain was once the stomping grounds of artists, writers, and intellectuals and the locus of café society. Café life, always important in Paris, has been vital in St-Germain. Verlaine and Rimbaud drank themselves into poetic exaltation here. At the Café de Flore and Les Deux Magots, Sartre, de Beauvoir, and Camus developed their existentialist philosophies, often over coffee and endless cigarettes. Today, St-Germain remains the hub of the French publishing industry, but the writers and artists of the neighborhood are very well heeled. The elegant streets have been taken over by cutting-edge interior design showrooms and art galleries. High-profile fashion designers dot the landscape with their chic, artistic boutiques, making the district one of the finest for shopping. The upscale hip and cultural sophisticates mix with artists and intellectuals in this quarter where literati meet glitterati.

PLACES TO SEE
Landmarks:

The quarter takes its name from the medieval abbey around which it rose: **St-Germain-des-Prés (1)** *(3 pl. St-Germain-des-Prés, 6th, 01-55.42.81.33)* is the oldest church in Paris, dating from 542; it became a Benedictine abbey in the 8th century. It was rebuilt and restored over the centuries; the present church dates from the 11th century. Outside, a Picasso sculpture, **Hommage to Apollinaire (2)** *(Rue de l'Abbaye and Pl. St-Germain-des-Prés, 6th)*, was created in dedication to the artist's friend, poet Guillaume Apollinaire. One of Paris's most romantic spots is the tiny square **Place de Furstenberg (3)**, a favorite film location. There, the home of 19th-century Romantic painter Eugène Delacroix is now the **Delacroix Museum (4)** *(6 rue de Furstenberg, 6th, 01-44.41.86.50, www.musee-delacroix.fr)*.

A result of Baron Haussmann's 19th-century urban planning, the wide, majestic **Blvd. St-Germain** is the main thoroughfare of the district. Replete with café terraces, restaurants, designer boutiques, and bookstores, the segment around the square of St-Germain is prime acreage for celebrity spottings. Some may be having a drink at one of the three most famous café-bars, noted for the writers, musicians, painters, and intellectuals that were regulars. In the 1920s and 1930s Hemingway, The Lost Generation, and the surrealists, followed in the 1950s by

existentialists, had their tables at **Les Deux Magots (5)** *(6 pl. St-Germain-des-Prés, 6th, 01-45.48.55.25, www.les deuxmagots.com)*. Poet Apollinaire held court at **Café de Flore (6)** *(172 bd. St-Germain, 6th, 01-45.48.55.26)*, claimed also by Sartre, Camus, and Simone de Beauvoir. Now the haunt of politicians and fashion designers, **Brasserie Lipp (7)** *(151 bd. St-Germain, 6th, 01-45.48. 53.91, www.brasserie-lipp.fr)* was once the meeting place for literary luminaries, such as Verlaine, Proust, Gide, and Malraux. Hemingway wrote *A Farewell to Arms* in this café; it has since been classified a historical monument. The next street westward, picturesque **Rue du Dragon (8)** *(6th)*, dates from the Middle Ages, and still has 17th- and 18th-century houses.

Explore the narrow streets of the quarter, full of eye-catching boutiques and art galleries, as you make your way southward to splendid **Place St-Sulpice**, dominated by the Fountain of the Four Bishops and pink-flowered chestnut trees. Another popular movie location is **Café**

de la Mairie. Construction of the church of **St-Sulpice (9)** *(Pl. St-Sulpice, 6th, 01-46.33.21.78)* took more than 100 years and is the result of the work of various architects.

The **Luxembourg Garden (10)** *(60 acres encircled by Bd. St-Michel, Rue de Médicis, Rue de Vaugirard, Rue Guynemer, and Rue August-*

Comte, 6th, 01-42.34.20.00) is Paris's most popular park. Formal terraces and wide walkways are adorned with statues of French queens. An octagonal pool, open-air café, puppet theatre, bandstand, and tennis courts are also among the features of this splendid park. The gardens sweep down from the Florentine-style royal palace **Palais du Luxembourg (11)** *(15 rue de Vaugirard, 6th, 01-42.34.20.00, www.senat.fr)*, now seat of the French Senate. Like the palace, the imposing 17th-century Baroque **Fontaine de Médicis (12)** *(15 rue de Vaugirard, 6th)*, to the east, was built for Marie de Médici, Florentine widow of Henri IV.

Take Rue de Vaugirard east to the **Théâtre National de l'Odéon (13)** *(1 pl. Paul-Claudel, 6th, 01-44.85.40.40, www.theatre-odeon.fr)*, once the home of the classical theatre company La Comédie Française. To the north, **Rue de l'Odéon**, lined with 18th-century houses and shops, is where, at No. 12, Sylvia Beach opened the original Shakespeare & Co. bookshop (1921-1940). Beach was friend and patron of writers such as F. Scott Fitzgerald, Ernest Hemingway, T.S. Eliot, and Ezra Pound. Largely thanks to her, James Joyce's *Ulysses* was first published in English. At the northern end of Rue de l'Odéon, on Blvd. St-Germain, is the **Carréfour de l'Odéon**, a square full of cinemas and student cafés—including Starbucks "de Paree"!

Cross Blvd. St-Germain and a few doors in on **Rue de**

l'Ancienne-Comédie is **Le Procope (14)** *(13 rue de l'Ancienne-Comédie, 6th, 01-40.46. 79.00, www.procope.com)*, the world's first café, established in 1686. Voltaire was said to drink 40 cups of coffee there every day; Napoleon was another frequent customer. In the next street over, **Cour du Commerce St-André**, at No. 9, Dr. Guillotin developed his "philanthropic decapitating machine." Around the corner is the charming and quaint 15th-century series of courtyards, **Cour de Rohan (15)** *(access from Rue du Jardinet and Blvd. St-Germain, 6th)*. The middle one has the only mounting block left in Paris, a *pas-de-mule* from which ladies and portly gentlemen mounted their mules.

Take Rue Mazarine all the way to the Seine and the **Institut de France (16)** *(23 quai de Conti, 6th, 01-44. 41.44.41, www.institut-de-france.fr)*, its majestic dome visible from afar. Home to five prestigious academies, the Institute's most famous group of scholars is the Académie Française, entrusted since 1635 with publishing the definitive French dictionary. Going west along the river, you reach the famous **School of Fine Arts (Beaux-Arts) (17)** *(13 quai Malaquais, 6th, 01-47.03.50.00, www.ensba.fr)*, where artists and architects the world over have been trained.

Arts & Entertainment:

Group tours of the **School of Fine Arts (Beaux-Arts) (17)** *(see also above, 01-47.03.52.15)* are by appointment only. The **Delacroix Museum (4)** *(see also page 125)* exhibits the painter's passionate canvases in his apartment and garden studio. The architectural mix of the abbey of **St-Germain-des-Prés (1)** *(see also page 125)* is noteworthy: 6th-century marble columns with Romanesque arches beneath Gothic vaults. A surviving original tower houses one of France's oldest belfries. The 17th-century philosopher René Descartes, among other notables, is buried here. If only in size, **St-Sulpice (9)** *(see also page 126)* would be very impressive; the work of 20 artists makes it unique. In the chapel right of the entrance are three fabulous murals by Delacroix. St-Germain-des-Prés and St-Sulpice also regularly hold concerts.

The **Théâtre du Vieux Colombier (18)** *(21 rue du Vieux-Colombier, 6th, 01-44.39.87.00)* one of the venues of the Comédie Française, presents French classics, notably the plays of Molière. The **Théâtre National de l'Odéon (13)** *(see also page 127)* specializes in foreign plays, in their original language. The work of Russian-born sculptor Ossip Zadkine is on display at the **Zadkine Museum (19)** *(100 bis, rue d'Assas, 6th, 01-43.26.91.90)*, where the artist lived and worked for nearly 40 years. The works cover his artistic development, from Cubism to Expressionism and Abstractionism.

PLACES TO EAT & DRINK
Where to Eat:

St-Germain is so full of good restaurants that it's best to leave the three literary landmark cafés, **Les Deux Magots (5)**, **Café de Flore (6)**, and **Brasserie Lipp (7)** *(see page 126)*, for drinks and people watching. For cheap and retro, the 1901 bistro **Le Petit St-Benoît (20)** **(€)** *(4 rue St-Benoît, 6th, 01-42.60.27.92)* is a hoot. Near the Beaux-Arts school and surrounded by art galleries, **La Palette (21)** **(€)** *(43 rue de Seine, 6th, 01-43.26.68.15)* is a neighborhood café full of students, art dealers, and artists. Great fish, wine, and Mediterranean food are part of the appeal of **Fish La Boissonnerie (22)** **(€-€€)** *(69 rue de Seine, 6th, 01-43.54.34.69)*. A best

buy is **Cosi (23)** **(€)** *(54 rue de Seine, 6th, 01-46.33.35.36)*, a fabulous sandwich shop. Japanese teppanyaki specialties, cooked in front of you, are exceptional at **Azabu (24)** **(€-€€)** *(3 rue André-Mazet, 6th, 01-46.33.72.05)*. The ghosts of Voltaire, Diderot, and Robespierre peer over your shoulder at Paris's oldest café-restaurant, **Le Procope (14)** **(€€€)** *(see also page 128)*.

Spit-roasted meats are the specialty at **La Rotisserie d'en Face (25)** **(€€€)** *(2 rue Christine, 6th, 01-43.26.40.98, www.jacques-cagna.com)*, frequented by businessmen and the chic alike. Eclectic food in a snazzy minimalist décor with an open, glass-paneled kitchen make a meal at **Ze Kitchen Galerie (26)** **(€€€)** *(4 rue des Grands-Augustins, 6th, 01-44.32.00.32)* an artistic experience. For the best

great names of the 1930s-1950s. The store and the clothing are appropriately high design at Lagerfeld Gallery (42) *(40 rue de Seine, 6th, 01-55.42.75.51)*, the designer's prêt-à-porter collection in a showroom decorated by hot Parisian interior designer Andrée Putman. The picturesque **open-air food market** at Rue de Buci (43) *(on Rue de Seine and Rue de Buci, from Blvd. St-Germain, 6th, daily except Mondays)* finds Parisians engaged in a favorite pastime. Exceptional pieces from the 1930s and 1940s are the crowning glory of Galerie Yves Gastou (44) *(12 rue Bonaparte, 6th, 01-53.73.00.10, www.galerieyvesgastou.com)*. La Maison Ivre (45) *(38 rue Jacob, 6th, 01-42.60.01.85)* stocks beautiful ceramics and linens from Provence. Unusual antiques at Yveline (46) *(4 rue Furstenberg, 6th, 01-43.26.56.91)* delight even the most experienced shopper.

Besides its beauty, **Blvd. St-Germain** is lined with great shops. The famous bookstore La Hune (47) *(170 bd. St-Germain, 6th, 01-45.48.35.85)* is known for its art, design, photography, and architecture books (in English and French), while its collection of fiction and critical works can keep you browsing 'til closing time at midnight. Façonnable (48) *(174 bd. St-Germain, 6th, 01-40.49.02.47)*, preppie with a fashionable French flair, is overwhelmingly men's wear but also has a line for women. Parisian chic means comfortable skinny knits for women and casual elegance

for men at Sonia Rykiel (49) *(Women: 175 bd. St-Germain, 6th, 01-49.54.60.60; Men: 194 bd. St-Germain, 6th, 01-49.54.60.96; www.soniarykiel.fr).* Rykiel Woman (50) *(4 rue de Grenelle, 6th, 01-49.54.66.21)* includes a range of intimate adult toys and accessories.

Lovely narrow streets south of Blvd. St-Germain—**Rue du Four**, **Rue de Rennes**, **Rue Bonaparte**, **Rue du Vieux-Colombier**, and the myriad criss-crossing streets—reveal a cornucopia of fashion designers and art galleries. Pastry chef extraordinaire Pierre Hermé (51) *(72 rue Bonaparte, 6th, 01-43.54.47.77)* treats his work like high-end fashion, by creating seasonal "collections." Those in the know line up for his creations. The glamorous, expensive lingerie at Sabbia Rosa (52) *(71-73 rue des Sts-Pères, 6th, 01-45.48.88.37)* is worthy of its French starlet clientele; items can be made to order. Shops along **Rue du Cherche-Midi** are especially inviting. The famous swimwear designs of Erès (53) *(4 bis, rue du Cherche-Midi, 6th, 01-45.44.95.54)* are simple and sophisticated. Robert Clergerie (54) *(5 rue du Cherche-Midi, 6th, 01-45.48.75.47)* offers beauty and comfort in practical daytime shoes. A few doors away Poilâne (55) *(8 rue du Cherche-Midi, 6th, 01-45.48.42.59, www.poilane.com)* continues to

make its famous bread, along with other bakery delights. On Sunday mornings (9 AM-1 PM) the organic market Marché Biologique (56) *(Bd. Raspail between Rue du Cherche-*

Midi and Rue de Rennes, 6th) is full of incredibly beautiful and delicious produce and products.

Leather designs in vibrant colors are the signature at Peggy Huyn Kinh (57) *(11 rue Coëtlogon, 6th, 01-42.84.83.83, www.peggy-huyn-kinh.fr)*. Longchamp (58) *(21 rue du Vieux-Colombier, 6th, 01-42.22.74.75)* doesn't stop at great handbags; its luggage collection is just as wonderful. Vanessa Bruno (59) *(25 rue St-Sulpice, 6th, 01-43.54.41.04)* designs—flattering, feminine, and sporty—are extremely popular. Daniel Jasiak (60) *(6 rue Cassette, 6th, 01-42.22.58.50)*, once a theatre costume designer, composes fashion in patchwork.

Master *chocolatier* Christian Constant (61) *(37 rue d'Assas, 6th, 01-53.63.15.15)* seeks inspiration around the globe for his creations. Way cool fashion for women and men at APC (62) *(3 & 4 rue de Fleurus, 6th, 01-42.22.12.77, www.apc.fr)*, designed by Jean Touitou, has followers all over Paris (past-season items are discounted at 45 rue Madame, 6th). Exceptional architecture and design books are the focus at Librairie le Moniteur (63) *(7 pl. de l'Odéon, 6th, 01-44.41.15.75, www.groupemoniteur.fr)*. The jewelry at Galerie Hélène Porée (64) *(1 rue de l'Odéon, 6th, 01-43.54.17.00, www.galerie-helene-poree.fr)* is truly wearable art. Le Mouton à Cinq Pattes (65) *(19 rue Grégoire-de-Tours, 6th, 01-43.29.73.56)* unearths vintage designer clothes and last season's numbers.

WHERE TO STAY

Famous 19th-century guests created delicious scandals at L'Hôtel (66) (€€€) *(13 rue des Beaux-Arts, 6th, 01-44.41.99.00, www.l-hotel.com)*; Oscar Wilde died there and music-hall star Mistinguett was a regular. Today, the luxurious hotel frequented by show-biz celebrities, is dramatic, flamboyant, and wonderful. Charming and well-managed, Hôtel Danube (67) (€-€€) *(58 rue Jacob, 6th, 01-42.60.94.07, www.hoteldanube.fr)* has spacious rooms in a mix of styles. A walled garden, wood-paneled rooms, and many small details make a stay at Hôtel St-Germain-des-Prés (68) (€€) *(36 rue Bonaparte, 6th, 01-43.26.00.19)* special.

Romantic, small, and charming Hôtel d'Angleterre (69) (€€) *(44 rue Jacob, 6th, 01-42.60.34.72, www.hotel-dangleterre.com)* welcomes guests warmly. A 17th-century townhouse with beamed ceilings and Aubusson tapestries, Hôtel d'Aubusson (70) (€€) *(33 rue Dauphine, 6th, 01-43.29.43.43)* is beautifully decorated. Dignified but not stuffy, Au Manoir St-Germain-des-Prés (71) (€€) *(153 bd. St-Germain, 6th, 01-42.22.21.65, toll-free in U.S. & Canada 800-528-1234, www.paris-hotels-charm.com)* has garden-themed common areas, large bedrooms, and Jacuzzis in the bathrooms. The Artus Hôtel (72) (€€) *(34 rue de Buci, 6th, 01-43.29.07.20, www.artushotel.com)*, with its zebra-patterned armchairs, stone fountain, and doors hand-painted by local artists, is unusual, imaginative, and chic, with simple, well-designed rooms.

Oriental rugs, tapestries, brocades, and arbors of blooming plants enhance the thick beams and stone walls of Grand Hôtel de l'Univers (73) (€€) *(6 rue Grégoire-de-Tours, 6th, 01-43.29.37.00, toll-free in U.S. 800-528-1234, www.hotel-paris-univers.com)*. Beautiful Le Madison Hôtel (74) (€€) *(143 bd. St-Germain, 6th, 01-40.51.60.00, www.hotel-madison.com)*—its sitting areas adorned with tapestries and antiques—combines modern amenities in the rooms with conventional furnishings, evoking the gracious charm of old inns. A great location and cheap prices make up for the small, worn-out rooms in the clean, unpretentious Welcome Hôtel (75) (€) *(66 rue de Seine, 6th, 01-46.34.24.80)*.

Oak beams, stone walls, Aubusson tapestries, and an abundance of fresh flowers give Hôtel Left Bank St-Germain (76) (€€) *(9 rue de l'Ancienne-Comédie, 6th, 01-43.54.01.70, toll-free in U.S. & Canada 800-528-1234, www.paris-hotels-charm.com)* much of its allure; the standard-size rooms are comfortable. Gracious common areas in the appealing Hôtel de Fleurie (77) (€€) *(32-34 rue Grégoire-de-Tours, 6th, 01-53.73.70.10, www.hotel-de-fleurie.fr)* are matched by rooms with a good layout and marble bathrooms. Location is the advantage of Atlantis St-Germain-des-Prés (78) (€€) *(4 rue du Vieux-Colombier, 6th, 01-45.48.31.81, www.hotelatlantis.com)*, across from St-Sulpice Church; clean rooms are decorated in a mix of Art Deco and traditional French. Nearby,

at spectacular **Hôtel de l'Abbaye (79)** (€€-€€€) *(10 rue Cassette, 6th, 01-45.44.38.11, www.hotel-abbaye.com),* once a 16th-17th-century convent, the cobblestone courtyard leads to a splendid reception and salon, while top-floor suites offer fireplaces, arched ceilings, and rooftop views. A super-cheap sleep across from the Luxembourg Gardens, **Pension Les Marronniers (80)** (€) *(78 rue d'Assas, 6th, 01-43.26.37.71, www.pension-marronniers.com)* is a fast-disappearing species, a pension with breakfast and dinner included; most bedrooms, basic and clean, share bathrooms.

RUE DU BAC

⑫ *to Solférino or Rue du Bac;* **⑩ ⑫** *to Sèvres-Babylone*

● SNAPSHOT ●

The Rue du Bac, an area of high-end design and fashion, is a slice of the Left Bank snuggled between sophisticated, hip St-Germain and refined, aristocratic Invalides. Elegant residential facades give a more sedate air to the neighborhood, though boutiques and restaurants claim the cream of French architectural and interior design—with names such as Philippe Starck, Andrée Putman, and Christian Biecher. The spectacular Musée d'Orsay is one of the highlights of this quarter.

PLACES TO SEE
Landmarks:

The **Quai Voltaire** has great river views of Concorde, the Tuileries Gardens, and the Louvre. Famous residents of the street include: Louise de Kéroualle, spy for Louis XIV, at Nos. 3–5; composers Richard Wagner and Jean Sibelius, poet Charles Baudelaire, and writer-pundit Oscar Wilde at No. 19; while No. 27 is where philosopher Voltaire died. Further east is the superb **Musée d'Orsay (81)** *(1 rue de la Légion-d'Honneur at Quai Anatole France, 7th, 01-40.49.48.14, www.musee-orsay.fr).* Once a train station, the building itself is as magnificent as the art it houses. Retaining much of the original architecture and ironwork, the museum's interior is lofty, airy, and spacious, the openness enhanced by wide exhibition spaces on multiple levels.

Rue du Bac is a classy street lined with elegant boutiques. The buildings and storefronts, many designed by France's top interior decorators, are as fascinating to look at as the wares inside. At the southern end of Rue du Bac, you come to **Le Bon Marché (82)** *(24 rue de Sèvres, 7th, 01-44.39.80.00, www.lebonmarche.fr)*, Paris's first department store. Designed by Gustave Eiffel, creator of the Eiffel Tower, the *fin-de-siècle* and Art Deco decoration of this landmark inspire some of the awe that Paris wins and deserves.

Arts & Entertainment:

The **Musée d'Orsay (81)** *(see also page 139)* houses a stunning collection of Impressionist paintings, Art Nouveau pieces, mid-to-late-19th-century works, and late-19th-century through early-20th-century paintings and sculptures. Architectural reproductions cover a wide range of styles represented in Parisian buildings. The **Musée Maillol (83)** *(59-61 rue de Grenelle, 7th, 01-42.22.59.58, www.museemaillol.com)* contains the artist's remarkable voluptuous sculptures and his other works, from drawings and engravings to paintings. It

also includes works of artists, such as Rodin, Picasso, and Cézanne. A hot Parisian venue for alternative international films, **La Pagode (84)** *(57 bis, rue de Babylone, 7th, 01-45.55.48.48)* escaped demolition in the 1970s as a result of the efforts by film director Louis Malle.

PLACES TO EAT & DRINK
Where to Eat:

If the jet-set bistro **Le Voltaire (85)** (€€€) *(27 Quai Voltaire, 7th, 01-42.61.17.49)* makes your head spin, the much more affordable café next door, "Le Petit Voltaire," serves delicious soups and omelettes. The museum restaurant, **Restaurant du Musée d'Orsay (86)** (€€) *(1 rue du Légion d'Honneur, 7th, 01-45.49.47.03)* offers lunch and tea in a spectacular setting with a magnificent view. For a light meal, the tearoom **Les Nuits des Thés (87)** (€) *(22 rue de Beaune, 7th, 01-47.03.92.07)* is pleasant and relaxing. The old-fashioned refinement of the quarter's dignified upper crust is reflected in the décor and menu at **La Calèche (88)** (€€) *(8 rue de Lille, 7th, 01-42.60.24.76)*.

With a no-reservations policy, it's a wait getting into the culinary hot spot **L'Atelier de Joël Robuchon (89)** (€€€) *(5 rue de Montalembert, 7th, 01-42.22.56.56)*, but it's worth it: you sit at u-shaped counters and taste tapas—like morsels of food for the gods. The soufflés are exceptional at **La Cigale (90)** (€€) *(11 bis, rue Chomel, 7th, 01-45.48.87.87)*. French standards prepared in large portions by the motherly owner of **Au Babylone (91)** (€) *(13 rue de Babylone, 7th, 01-45.48.72.13)* satisfy anyone's nostalgia for typical French lunches of the past.

Audacious, light, clever, out of this world—these are some of the ways people describe the surprising, delicious creations of chef-owner Claude Colliot at **Le Bamboche (92) (€€€)** *(15 rue de Babylone, 7th, 01-45.49.14.40)*. The in-store café at Le Bon Marché, **Delicabar (93) (€-€€)** *(Le Bon Marché, 1st floor, 26 rue de Sèvres, 7th, 01-42.22.10.12, www.delicabar.fr)*, designed by Claudio Colucci and featuring an open courtyard terrace, serves sweet and savory delicacies: try the delectable chocolate *foie gras*!

Reserve in advance to get into a place everyone raves about: **L'Epi Dupin (94) (€€)** *(11 rue Dupin, 6th, 01-42.22.64.56)*, near the Bon Marché, serves refined versions of bistro classics in a friendly atmosphere (though it gets hectic at rush hours, the consensus is it's worth it). The *crêperie* **Le Goémon (95) (€)** *(11 rue Oudinot, 7th, 01-42.73.35.17)* is a hidden treasure. Another fabulous cheap eat is **Restaurant Chez Germaine (96) (€)** *(30 rue Pierre-Leroux, 7th, 01-42.73.28.34)*, whose homespun food is rich and authentic.

Bars & Nightlife:
This quiet, refined quarter tends to close shop early. St-Germain is more conducive to nightlife.

WHERE TO SHOP

Take to the streets and browse the many *antiquaires* in this quarter. The shops of Carré Rive Gauche (97) *(bordered by Quai Voltaire, Rue des St-Pères, Rue de l'Université, and Rue du Bac)*, an association of antique dealers, carry quality items from the grandiose to the rustic. The cashmere wonders of designer Lucien Pellat-Finet (98) *(1 rue Montalembert, 7th, 01-42.22.22.77)* are perfectly suited to the décor created by hot interior designer Christian Biecher. The 1940s look is the thing at Corrine Sarrut (99) *(4 rue du Pré-aux-Clercs, 7th, 01-42.61.71.60)*, who designed Audrey Tautou's costumes for the film *Amélie*. Connoisseurs know the chocolates magnificently displayed at Debauve & Gallais (100) *(30 rue des Sts-Pères, 7th, 01-45.48.54.67, www.debauve-et-gallais.com)* are among the most divine; you can order online from abroad. Alain Mikli (101) *(74 rue des Sts-Pères, 7th, 01-53.63.87.40, www.mikli.fr)* carries the designer's signature eyeglasses as well as his funky, futuristic ready-to-wear collection and handbags. Exquisite chocolates at Richart (102) *(258 bd. St-Germain, 7th, 01-45.55.66.00, www.richart.com)* come with tips on chocolate appreciation.

The signature cuts and finishes of Yohji Yamamoto (103) *(3 rue de Grenelle, 7th, 01-42.84.28.87)* are inspired by the kimono. Nine perfume-makers have created the unique, complex scents at Editions de Parfums Frédéric Malle (104) *(37 rue de Grenelle, 7th, 01-42.22.77.22, www.editionsdeparfums.com)*.

The famous French interior designer Christian Liaigre (105) *(42 rue du Bac, 7th, 01-53.63.33.66)* has decorated hotels, stores, and restaurants in Paris and New York; here his furniture and lighting creations are sold. For four generations Ryst Dupeyron (106) *(79 rue du Bac, 7th, 01-45.48.80.93, www.ryst-dupeyron.com)* has sold *armagnac* and fine spirits, with bottled treasures dating from 1868.

Le Bon Marché (82) *(see also page 140)* is the most chic of all Parisian department stores. It offers the latest in designer fashions for both women and men, as well as its own (less expensive) brand. The food hall, **La Grande Épicerie**, presents luscious displays in a grand setting.

WHERE TO STAY

If your priority is peace and quiet, this sedate neighborhood might be just the thing. Understated, tasteful rooms at Hôtel d'Orsay (107) (€€) *(93 rue de Lille, 7th, 01-47.05.85.54, www.esprit-de-france.com)* are warmly decorated and reasonably priced. Clean and quiet, Hôtel Bersoly's St-Germain (108) (€) *(28 rue de Lille, 7th, 01-42.60.73.79, www.bersolyshotel.com)* offers basic amenities. In a 17th-century building with original cross beams and stone walls, the small, charming Hôtel Verneuil (109) (€) *(8 rue de Verneuil, 7th, 01-42.60. 82.14, www.hotelverneuil.com)* is run by an art collector who has made it her mission to make you feel like a guest in her home.

The budget-conscious can still spend the night in this tiny quarter: though it hasn't seen renovations in decades, Hôtel de l'Université (110) (€-€€) *(22 rue de* l'Université, 7th, 01-42.61.09.39, www.hoteluniversite.com) does offer huge, comfortable rooms with fraying vintage furnishings; two rooms are *sans* toilet. An arty crowd appreciates the Art Deco lobby with its elephant and panther statues, as well as the jazz bar at **Hôtel Lenox St-Germain (111)** (€-€€) *(9 rue de l'Université, 7th, 01-42.96.10.95, www.lenoxsaintgermain.com)*; rooms are more classically furnished.

Rooms at the elegant **Le Montalembert (112)** (€€€) *(3 rue Montalembert, 7th, 01-45.49.68.68)* vary enormously in style, from contemporary chic to Louis-Philippe pomp. Simple, smart, and well-designed, **Hôtel St-Thomas-d'Aquin (113)** (€) *(3 rue Pré-aux-Clercs, 7th, 01-42.61.01.22, www.hotel-st-thomas-daquin.com)* is an excellent deal; therefore, usually booked.

Sumptuous and distinguished, the luxurious Regency-styled **Hôtel Duc de Saint-Simon (114)** (€€-€€€) *(14 rue de St-Simon, 7th, 01-44.39.20.20, www.hotelducdesaintsimon.com)* caters to a discerning clientele. At the grand Left Bank establishment **Hôtel Lutétia (115)** (€€€) *(45 bd. Raspail, 6th, 01-49.54.46.46)*, the rooms are plush, the hallways graced with statues, and the service impeccable.

MONTPARNASSE

④ ⑥ ⑫ ⑬ *to Montparnasse-Bienvenüe;* ④ *to Vavin;*
⑥ *to Edgar Quinet;* ⑬ *to Gaîté;*
④ ⑥ *to Raspail or Denfert-Rochereau*

• SNAPSHOT •

Montparnasse was once the neighborhood of illustrious artists: Picasso, Léger, Soutine, Braque, Modigliani, Chagall, Zadkine, and Man Ray lived there, as did writers Gertrude Stein, Henry Miller, and Ezra Pound. Between the two World Wars it was the symbol of modernity, a hotbed of intellectual and artistic creativity. Those days are long gone. The first Parisian skyscraper, the Tour Montparnasse, caused horror in the 1970s, resulting in changes in building regulations for central Paris. The area has unfortunately suffered from tragic urban development policies, but it's worth a trip just to visit the haunts of some of the 20th century's great cultural and artistic figures.

PLACES TO SEE
Landmarks:

The **Tour Montparnasse (116)** *(Pl. Raoul Dautry, 14th, 01-45.38.52.56)* was the biggest office building in Europe when it was built in 1973. An observation deck on the 56th floor provides good views of the city. Below, the café-restaurant **La Coupole (117)** *(102 bd. du Montparnasse, 14th, 01-43.20.14.20)* has had a famous artistic clientele, including Jean-Paul Sartre, Josephine

Baker, and Roman Polanski. **La Closerie des Lilas (118)** *(171 bd. du Montparnasse, 14th, 01-40.51.34.50)* was the favorite café-bar of Hemingway, F. Scott Fitzgerald, Lenin, and Trotsky. The café is practically a character in Hemingway's novel *The Sun Also Rises*, which he wrote on the terrace in six weeks. Art Deco buildings ornament **Rue Campagne-Première (119)** *(14th)*, the street where many artists lived between the two World Wars; among them, Picasso, Kandinsky, and Joan Miró. Modigliani, suffering from tuberculosis and opium addiction, lived in No. 3.

The **Montparnasse Cemetery (120)** *(3 bd. Edgar-Quinet, 14th, 01-44.10.86.50)*, commissioned by Napoleon, is the resting place of many famous writers and artists. Among them are: Samuel Beckett, Charles Baudelaire, Jean-Paul Sartre, Simone de Beauvoir, Guy de Maupassant, Tristan Tzara, Eugene Ionesco, Constantin Brancusi, Frédéric Bartholdi (sculptor of the Statue of Liberty), Man Ray, Chaïm Soutine, Jean Seberg, Camille Saint-Saëns, André Citroën, Serge Gainsbourg, and Henri Laurens.

Beneath the streets of Paris runs a 3,000-km network of tunnels (nearly 2,000 miles). During World War II the passages were used by the Resistance; in 1968, by demonstrating students evading the cops. In one of these spaces, just before the French Revolution, the bones of six million Parisians were transferred by wheelbarrow from overcrowded cemeteries within the city and dumped into the **Catacombs (121)** *(1 pl.*

Denfert-Rochereau, 14th, 01-43.22.47.63). During the Reign of Terror, more bodies were dumped there. The bones of Marat, Robespierre, and other French citizens are packed in layer upon layer of skulls and bones, all on public display some 25 yards below the streets of the city.

Arts & Entertainment:

The Musée du Montparnasse (122) *(21 ave. du Maine, 15th, 01-42.22.91.96)* captures the ethos of the early 20th century's bohemian quarter in what used to be a hangout for Montparnasse artists such as Picasso, Modigliani, and Chagall. The Fondation Henri Cartier-Bresson (123) *(2 impasse Lebouis, 14th, 01-56.80.27.00, www.henricartierbresson.org)* is a museum dedicated to the works of the great French photographer. The Fondation Cartier pour l'Art Contemporain (124) *(261 bd. Raspail, 14th, 01-42.18.56.72, www.fondation. cartier.fr)*, a center for contemporary art, theatre, music, and dance, is housed in a spectacular glass building designed by Jean Nouvel. Depending on how the sun hits it, passersby can either catch a glimpse of the exhibits inside, or see reflections of the busy urban surroundings along the boulevard.

PLACES TO EAT & DRINK
Where to Eat:

Montparnasse was a social hub for early 20th-century artists and writers. It was common to sight the likes of Picasso, Modigliani, Cocteau, Apollinaire, Hemingway, F. Scott Fitzgerald, and many others along Boulevard du Montparnasse—especially in the two favorite café-bar-restaurants. The literati are long gone, but the restaurants remain. You can only imagine discussing feminism with Simone de Beauvoir over an *apéritif* at the Art Deco-styled **La Coupole (117)** (€€-€€€) (*102 bd. du Montparnasse, 14th, 01-43.20.14.20, www.lacoupoleparis.com*). Today, one goes there because of its illustrious history, not for the food; drinks will do the trick just as well. On the other hand, **Le Dôme (125)** (€€€) (*108 bd. du Montparnasse, 14th, 01-43.35.25.81*), that other Montparnasse institution, offers fabulous fish and seafood in an equally superb Art Deco interior.

In a street full of *crêperies*, don't miss the magnificent **Crêperie de Josselin (126)** (€) (*67 rue du Montparnasse, 14th, 01-43.20.93.50*); lovely, romantic, and as relaxed as the Breton countryside, the whole experience is most satisfying. If you have a hankering for Italian, **Auberge de Venise (127)** (€€) (*10 rue Delambre, 14th, 01-43.35.43.09*) assures exceptional food in a comfortable ambience.

In the tiny, classic bistro **Chez Marcel (128)** (€€) (*7 rue Stanislas, 6th, 01-45.48.29.94*) you feel like you're a guest in the chef's home: good Lyonnais cuisine is matched by friendly service and down-home décor. Imaginative bistro fare and a great wine list put **Wadja (129)** (€€) (*10 rue de la Grande-Chaumière,*

6th, 01-46.33.02.02) on the "good value" list. **Le Caméléon (130) (€€)** *(6 rue de Chevreuse, 6th, 01-43.20.63.43)* is an old-fashioned bistro—homey with unpretentious classic French food. A good cheap eat is **Class'Croûte (131) (€)** *(156 bd. Montparnasse, 14th, 01-56.54.85.48, www.classcroute.com)*, which offers sandwiches, salads, pastas, and savory tarts.

Bars & Nightlife:

Watch the world go by at the famous café-bars on **Blvd. du Montparnasse**: **La Coupole (117)** *(No. 102, see page 146)*, **Le Dôme (125)** *(No. 108, see page 149)*, or **Le Select (132)** *(99 bd. du Montparnasse, 6th, 01-45.48.38.24)*. The **Fondation Cartier (124)** *(see also page 148)* hosts very hip arts soirées. **Rosebud (133)** *(11 bis, rue Delambre, 14th, 01-43.35.38.54)*, a 1950s-style café-bar, attracts a chic, more mature (30ish to 50ish), arty and media crowd with its retro glamour.

WHERE TO SHOP

The **open-air food market** at Rue Daguerre **(134)** *(between ave. du Maine and ave. du Général-Leclerc, 14th)* is a daily feast. But food isn't the only offering here: Divine **(135)** *(39 rue Daguerre, 14th, 01-43.22.28.10, Tues.-Sat.)* sells berets, hats, scarves, and gloves for men and

women. Adorable outfits for children, linens, lace, robes, nightgowns, cosmetics, and food products, all made by nuns and monks throughout France, are sold at La Boutique

The fabulous architecture is capped by the famous ovoid dome, the second highest point in Paris after the Eiffel Tower.

West of the basilica is the **Place du Tertre (6)** *(18th)*, full of quick-draw portraitists and swamped with tourists. Another Montmartre legend is that the term "bistro" originated here in the early 1800s when Russian soldiers in the restaurant **La Mère Catherine** shouted "Bistro!" ("Quickly!") for faster service. Northward, the cabaret **Au Lapin Agile (7)** *(22 rue des Saules, 18th, 01-46. 06.85.87)* retains its early 20th-century atmosphere when it was a favorite of artists and poets. Of the old village windmills, two remain, both in Rue Lepic: Moulin du Radet (further down) and **Moulin de la Galette (8)** *(Rue Lepic and rue Tholoze, 18th)*, which became a dancehall that inspired work by Vincent van Gogh and Auguste Renoir. Many painters lived and had studios in tranquil **Avenue Junot (9)** *(18th)*. Nearby on a lovely square, **Le Bateau-Lavoir (10)** *(13 pl. Emile-Goudeau, 18th)* was a neglected, run-down building of artists' studios and apartments shared in the early 1900s by Modigliani, Picasso, Braque, Juan Gris, and Marie Laurencin, among others. Here, in 1907, Picasso painted *Les Demoiselles d'Avignon*, considered the painting that launched Cubism. Now rebuilt, this historical building again provides studio and living space for emerging artists.

Arts & Entertainment:

The **Max Fourny Museum of Naïf Art (11)** *(Halle St-Pierre, 2 rue Ronsard, 18th, 01-42.58.72.89, www.hallesaint pierre.org)* contains paintings and sculptures from more than 30 countries. Near the Place du Tertre, the **Espace Montmartre Salvador Dali (12)** *(11 rue Poulbot, 18th, 01-42.64.40.10)* exhibits the Surrealist artist's work. The **Musée de Montmartre (13)** *(12 rue Cortot, 18th, 01-46.06.61.11)* covers the history of Montmartre and its bohemian life, and includes a reconstruction of the Café de l'Abreuvoir, Utrillo's favorite café.

The art cinema **Studio 28 (14)** *(10 rue Tholozé, 18th, 01-46.06.36.07, www.cinemastudio28.com)* was decorated by Jean Cocteau. The **Théâtre de l'Atelier (15)** *(1 pl. Charles-Dullin, 18th, 01-46.06.49.24, www.theatre-atelier.com)* stages contemporary plays, both French and international.

PLACES TO EAT & DRINK
Where to Eat:

In an area that's a known tourist trap, **Le Maquis (16)** *(€-€€)* *(69 rue Caulaincourt, 18th, 01-42.59.76.07)* is a good neighborhood restaurant serving traditional dishes prepared with fresh, seasonal ingredients. **Le Moulin de la Galette (17)** *(€€-€€€)* *(83 rue Lepic, 18th, 01-46.06.84.77)*, by the famous

 windmill, is a stunning, romantic locale with delectable food. A trendy, artistic Montmartre crowd converges on **Le Soleil**

Gourmand (18) (€) *(10 rue Ravignan, 18th, 01-42.51.00.50)*: the food is simple; the ambience outstanding. Also super-hip is **Café Burq (19)** (€€) *(6 rue Burq, 18th, 01-42.52.81.27)*, with terrific New French Bistro fare, a great atmosphere, and music to match.

A talented Basque chef with culinary inspiration from Southeast Asia, Latin America, North Africa, and France has a hit on his hands: **La Famille (20)** (€€) *(41 rue des Trois-Frères, 18th, 01-42.52.11.12)* is one of the trendiest Parisian restaurants. The atmosphere is relaxed with a friendly and cool crowd, and good music to boot. Cheap, cheap, cheap: **Claude et Nicole (21)** (€) *(13 rue des Trois-Frères, 18th, 01-46.06.12.48)* isn't haute anything; its simple, good, inexpensive food comes in large portions. **L'Entracte (22)** (€€) *(44 rue d'Orsel, 18th, 01-46.06.93.41)*, a tiny, intimate bistro, does classic French dishes very well.

Bars & Nightlife:

For songs of the good old days, the cabaret **Au Lapin Agile (7)** *(see also page 157)* has just the right touch of nostalgia. Play chess, backgammon, or Scrabble at the friendly, funky café **Chez Camille (23)** *(8 rue Ravignan, 18th, 01-46.06.05.78)*. **Doudingue (24)** *(24 rue Durantin, 18th, 01-42.54.88.08)* means "crazy but nice," apt for this bar furnished with a mix of Baroque, Oriental, and flea market; DJs spin discs and there's a menu of health food.

Hand-painted scarves, bags, and belts by Amaya Eguizabal (25) *(45 rue Lepic, 18th, 01-44.92.91.46)* are works of art. Young, avant-garde designers Fanche et Flo (26) *(19 rue Durantin, 18th, 01-42.51.24.18)* create bold clothing, objects, jewelry, lighting, and furniture. Designer children's clothes at Gaspard de la Butte (27) *(10 bis, rue Yvonne-le-Tac, 18th, 01-42.55.99.40, www.gasparddelabutte.com)* are beautiful, fanciful, and imaginative. Modern designs in glass, ceramics, and lighting are fabulous at Pages 50/70: Olivier Verlet (28) *(15 rue Yvonne-le-Tac, 18th, 01-42.52.48.59)*.

Rue d'Orsel is full of wonderful boutiques, such as Zelia sur la Terre comme au Ciel (29) *(47 ter, rue d'Orsel, 18th, 01-46.06.96.51, www.zelia.net)*, an extravagant, imaginative wedding shop. Look for high-design furniture and objects at Galerie Christine Diegoni (30) *(47 ter, rue d'Orsel, 18th, 01-42.64.69.48)*, and exuberant lighting fixtures at David Emery Creation (31) *(52 rue d'Orsel, 18th, 01-55.79.76.56, www.davidemerycreation.com)*. Senteurs de Fée (32) *(47 bis, rue d'Orsel, 18th, 01-42.52.25.98)* stocks incense. Belle de Jour (33) *(7 rue Tardieu, 18th, 01-46.06.15.28)* has every imaginable crystal perfume bottle.

Marché St-Pierre (34) *(Rue Charles-Nodier, Place St-Pierre, 18th)* is the place to go for fabrics and trimmings; many shops offer discounted remnants. Emerging designers favor **Rue des Gardes**. No. 6 (35) *(a shop with no name, 6 rue des Gardes, 18th)* showcases fabulous, not-to-be-missed new designers. Beautifully lined, bright leather bags by Luc Dognin (36) *(4 rue des Gardes, 18th, 01-44.92.32.16)* are the rage all over Paris. Lily Latifi (37) *(11 rue des Gardes, 18th, 01-42.23.30.86, www.lily latifi.com)* meshes industrial design with applied and visual arts to create unusual fabrics that she turns into objects, clothing, and bags.

WHERE TO STAY

Exhibitions by local artists and magnificent views are some of the highlights of the formal but not pretentious Terrass Hôtel (38) (€€-€€€) *(12 rue Joseph-de-Maistre, 18th, 01-46.06.72.85, www.terrass-hotel.com)*. You get value for money at the quiet, clean, family-run Hôtel des Arts (39) (€) *(5 rue Tholozé, 18th, 01-46.06.30.52, www.arts-hotel-paris.com)*. It's quite an uphill hike from the métro, but the views are spectacular at the romantic, antique-filled Ermitage Hôtel (40) (€) *(24 rue Lamarck, 18th, 01-42.64.79.22)*.

2 12 *to Pigalle;* **2** *to Blanche or Anvers*

● SNAPSHOT ●

Pigalle, once the sleazy red-light center of Paris, has begun cleaning up its neighborhood of streetwalkers, peep shows, and erotic cabarets. That cabaret scene was immortalized in the posters that Toulouse-Lautrec made of characters and places in Pigalle. His renderings of *danseuse* Jane Avril at dancehalls such as the Moulin Rouge, the Divan Japonais, and Le Chat Noir, as well as his posters of *chansonnier* Aristide Bruant added atmosphere to the seediness of the quarter renowned for its brothels.

PLACES TO SEE
Landmarks:

Famous artists and infamous characters are buried in **Montmartre Cemetery (41)** *(20 ave. Rachel, 18th, 01-53.42.36.30)*: dancer Nijinsky, filmmaker Truffaut,

painter Degas, composers Berlioz and Offenbach, and writers Stendhal and Dumas *fils* lie beside La Goulue (Louise Weber, the first can-can performer and Toulouse-Lautrec's model), Alphonsine Plessis (consumptive inspiration for Dumas' *La Dame aux Camélias*), and famed beauty Madame de Récamier.

The **Moulin Rouge (42)** *(82 bd. de Clichy, 18th, 01-53.09.82.82, www.moulin rouge.fr)* was once a baudy, populist cabaret theatre. Today, while they still do the can-can there, it holds

none of the original naughty atmosphere but is instead an expensive, Las Vegas-style tourist trap.

Arts & Entertainment:

In keeping with its location among the sex shops and shows of Pigalle, the **Museum of Eroticism (43)** *(72 bd. de Clichy, 18th, 01-42.58.28.73, www.eroticmuseum.com)* focuses on sex as a motif of folk art. On display are phalluses, fertility symbols, figurines, pictures, and a history of Parisian brothels. Instructive and funny, at times seedy, it's not erotic in itself.

PLACES TO EAT & DRINK
Where to Eat:

Basic food in a funky décor (read: garage-sale furnishings) is what the family-owned **L'Homme Tranquille (44)** (€-€€) *(81 rue des Martyrs, 18th, 01-42.54.56.28)* offers. Locals know that **Chez Toinette (45)** (€) *(20 rue Germain Pilon, 18th, 01-42.54.44.36)* is a good deal: the young, arty clientele loves the fun, casual atmosphere and fills up on French home cooking. **Rose Bakery (46)** (€) *(46 rue des Martyrs, 9th, 01-42.82.12.80)* has all things English but is especially good for tea and dessert.

Bars & Nightlife:

Though the **Moulin Rouge (42)** *(see also page 163)* has become a cheesy venue catering to tourists, other cabarets have turned into hip clubs. **Rue des Martyrs** is a happening spot. Toulouse-Lautrec's Le Divan Japonais has become **Le Divan du Monde (47)** *(75 rue des Martyrs, 18th, 01-42.52.02.46, www.divandumonde.com)*, featuring a wide range of music, from hip-hop to Cuban, reggae to techno-pop, in a laid-back setting. At night the hip **La Fourmi (48)** *(74 rue des Martyrs, 18th, 01-42.64.70.35)* attracts both party-till-dawners and casual drinkers, goths, and the flannel-shirted set.

WHERE TO SHOP

Industrial objects and furnishings seem like art at Gilles Oudin Métiers d'Art et d'Industrie (49) *(20 ave. de Trudaine, 9th, 01-48.74.04.24)*. Cutting-edge design characterizes **Rue des Martyrs**. Vintage French 1950s-1970s objects and furnishings make Et puis c'est tout (50) *(72 rue des Martyrs, 9th, 01-40.23.94.02)* stand out. Inspired by 1930s music-halls, photographs, and flea markets, the stylish bags of Emmanuelle Zysman (51) *(81 rue des Martyrs, 18th, 01-42.52.01.00)* are sold around the world. Elegance is the by-word at Heaven (52) *(83 rue des Martyrs, 18th, 01-44.92.92.92, www.heaven-paris.com)*, where a fashion designer and lighting creator have teamed up to showcase their works. Simple, unique, and beautiful, Patricia Louisor (53) *(16 rue Houdon, 18th, 01-42.62.10.42)* clothes are "for working, dancing, or seduction." Architectural lines in soft, luxurious fabrics give the clothes at FuturWare

OUTSKIRTS OF PARIS

PLACES TO SEE:

1. Bois de Boulogne
2. Parc André Citroën
3. Bois de Vincennes
4. Père Lachaise Cemetery
5. Belleville/Ménilmontant
6. Parc des Buttes-Chaumont
7. Parc de la Villette: City of Science; City of Music
8. Flea Market of St-Ouen
9. La Grande Arche de la Défense

I could spend my whole life
watching the Seine flow by...
It is a poem of Paris.

—*Blaise Cendrars*

At the farther reaches of Paris are a number of notable spots that make for a lovely few hours or even a whole day. Although exploring these areas is recommended, it is not advisable to walk around the parks at night. These areas are at some distance from the main attractions of the city, so it is preferable to find a hotel in central Paris rather than in such outlying spots.

BOIS DE BOULOGNE (1) *(16th)*

2 *to Porte Dauphine;* **1** *to Porte Maillot or Les Sablons;* **10** *to Porte d'Auteuil*

West of Paris is the **Bois de Boulogne**, a stunning park of more than 2,000 acres. Once the royal hunting grounds, it is a magical forest with gardens, woods, lakes, châteaux, and racetracks, an idyllic place for walking, boating, bicycling, and other outdoor recreation. To tour the vast grounds, rent a bicycle near **Pavillon Royal** *(Route de Suresnes)*, a short walk from the Art Nouveau métro station **Porte Dauphine** *(M: 2)*. Among the features of the Bois are the **Jardin d'Acclimatation** *(01-40.67.90.82, www.jardindacclimatation.fr)*, a children's amusement park; the **Parc de Bagatelle** *(Route de Sèvres à Neuilly)*, a park and château; and the romantic garden **Pré Catelan**, site also of a famous restaurant. The **Shakespeare Garden** contains flowers, trees, and plants that appear in the poet's plays, as well as an open-air theatre. Two lakes, **Lac Supérieur** and **Lac Inférieur**, offer boating opportunities. France's two most famous horseracing tracks, **Hippodrome de Longchamp** (*Route des Tribunes, 01-44.30.75.00*) and **Hippodrome d'Auteuil** (*Route des Lacs, 01-40.71.47.47*), are located in the Bois. The **Stade Roland-Garros** (*Porte des Mousquetaires, 2 ave. Gordon-Bennett, 01-47.43.48.00, www.fft.fr/rolandgarros/fr*) hosts the annual French Open Tennis Championships (late May-early June). Kings kept their mistresses in châteaux in the Bois de Boulogne, giving the park its reputation for love; today, night brings out transsexuals and swingers of all sorts.

The French gastronomic treasure **Le Pré Catelan** (€€€) (*Route de Suresnes, 16th, 01-44.14.41.14, www. lenotre.fr*) serves exquisite French cuisine in a romantic setting. There are numerous restaurants (mostly elegant and expensive) and cafés in the park. A boat ride and enchanting outdoor setting enhance the dining experience at **Le Chalet des Iles** (€€€) (*on the larger island of* **Lac Inférieur**, *01-42.88.04.69, www.chaletdesiles.net*).

PARC ANDRÉ CITROËN (2) *(15th)*

8 *to Balard;* 10 *to Javel/André-Citroën*

Parc André Citroën (*08-20.00.75.75*), built on the grounds of the old Citroën car factory, is a marvel of landscape architecture. Greenhouses, ponds, fountains, gardens, and inventive formations of hedges and trees blend into a wonderland of primitive and formal nature.

① *to Château de Vincennes;*
⑧ *to Porte de Charenton or Porte Dorée*

Like the Bois de Boulogne, the **Bois de Vincennes** *(www.boisdevincennes.com)* was once a royal hunting ground. On the southeast edge of Paris, it is home to a famous zoo, a floral garden, racetrack, château and fortress, and various sports and horticultural sites. Along the north side, the **Château de Vincennes** *(entry by the Tour du Village 1, ave. de Paris, 01-48.08.31.20)*, a medieval fortified castle, has been a royal residence, prison, porcelain factory, and arsenal. The **castle keep** is the château's museum. Nearby is **Parc Floral** *(01-43.43.92.95, www.parcfloraldeparis.com)*, a botanic garden. The three lakes—**Lac des Minimes**, **Lac Daumesnil**, and **Lac de Gravelle**—are beautiful areas for walking and boating. In the **Parc Zoologique** *(Ave. de St-Maurice, 01-44.75.20.10)* animals roam freely within large enclosures resembling their natural habitats. The Bois also houses the **Buddhist Temple of Paris** *(Route de la Ceinture du Lac Daumesnil, 01-40.04.98.06, www.kagyu-dzong.org)* and the **Aquarium of Tropical Fish** *(293 ave. Daumesnil, 01-44.74.84.80, www.palais-portedoree.org).*

Deep within the Bois is the **Cartoucherie de Vincennes**

 (Route du Champ de Manoeuvre; from Métro Château de Vincennes, free shuttle bus, or bus 112); once a munitions warehouse, it became home to some of the world's best

avant-garde theatre during the politically turbulent 1960s. Most famous of the five troupes housed there, the **Théâtre du Soleil** *(01-43.74.87.63, www.theatre-du-soleil.fr)* is a must-see for anyone interested in theatre. The troupe creates grand political epics using masks, puppets, and musicians, and drawing on international theatre traditions. The other troupes are also inspiring: **Théâtre de l'Aquarium** *(01-43.74.99.61, www.theatrede laquarium.com)*; **Théâtre de la Tempête** *(01-43.28.36.36, www.la-tempete.fr)*; **Théâtre de l'Epée de Bois** *(01-48.08.39.74)*; and **Théâtre du Chaudron** *(01-43.28.97.04)*.

In the park there is a **café** (on **Reuilly Island** in Lac Daumesnil) and a **restaurant** (on **Porte Jaune Island** in Lac des Minimes). Theatrical productions at the **Cartoucherie** have the bonus of good food in the **lobby cafés**: the soup, bread, and sandwiches are homemade. Excellent classical cuisine (seafood, seasonal game) can be expected at **Au Pressoir (€€€)** *(257 ave. Daumesnil, 12th, 01-43.44.38.21)*; leather armchairs and oak paneling add refinement. A tiny treasure in a former butcher shop, **Les Zygomates (€€)** *(7 rue de Capri, 12th, 01-40. 19.93.04)* serves excellent cuisine with a flair. Great Gascon food at the homey **Au Trou Gascon (€€€)** *(40 rue Taine, 12th, 01-43.44.34.26)* includes *foie gras* and *cassoulet*. Good game is on the menu in hunting season at **La Sologne (€€)** *(164 ave. Daumesnil, 12th, 01-43.07. 68.97)*; otherwise traditional French tempts the appetite in lovely, exposed-stone décor.

PÈRE LACHAISE CEMETERY (4) *(20th)*

②③ *to Père Lachaise;* **②** *to Philippe Auguste*

Paris's most famous and most prestigious cemetery, **Père Lachaise** *(16 rue du Repos, at bd. de Ménilmontant, 20th, 01-55.25.82.10)*, set on a wooded hill, is full of beautiful tombstones and funerary sculptures. Famous people interred here include Proust, Delacroix, Edith Piaf, Colette, Chopin, Balzac, Sarah Bernhardt, Oscar Wilde, Simone Signoret and Yves Montand, Alfred de Musset, Molière, La Fontaine, Abélard and Héloïse, Jim Morrison, Gertrude Stein and Alice B. Toklas, Richard Wright, Isadora Duncan, and Baron Haussmann.

The décor is run down, but the food and atmosphere at **Bistrot des Capucins** *(€€) (27 ave. Gambetta, 20th, 01-46.36.74.75)* are delightful. The cozy, intimate West African restaurant **Waly Fay** *(€€) (6 rue Godefroy-Cavaignac, 11th, 01-40.24.17.79, M: 9 to Charonne)* serves perfumed spicy stews and other delicacies in an elegant, warm ambience.

The retro music bar-café **Le Piston Pélican** *(15 rue de Bagnolet, 20th, 01-43.70.35.00)*, with its atmospheric vintage bar and dining area resembling a train station waiting room, attracts a hip young crowd. In what was once a railway station, the trendy bar **La Flèche d'Or** *(102 bis, rue de Bagnolet, 20th, 01-43.72.04.23, www.flechedor.com)* gives free concerts on weeknights (6 PM).

BELLEVILLE/MÉNILMONTANT (5) *(20th)*

② **⑪** *to Belleville;* **②** *to Couronnes or Ménilmontant;*
⑪ *to Pyrénées or Jourdain*

Belleville and **Ménilmontant**, the hilly area between Père Lachaise Cemetery and the Parc des Buttes-Chaumont, has seen a succession of some 60 different immigrant populations over the years, giving it a lively, diverse character. Edith Piaf, the torch singer who rose from poverty to international fame, was born at 72 rue de Belleville. Piaf memorabilia are gathered at the **Edith Piaf Museum** *(5 rue Crespin-du-Gast, 11th, 01-43.55.52.72, by appt. only)*. Another famous neighborhood figure was singer and film star Maurice Chevalier. With artists and young Parisians increasingly claiming the turf, this fascinating quarter has gentrified significantly. Artists—painters, photographers, jewelers, musicians—open their studios to the public every year in mid-May at the **Portes Ouvertes** event, sponsored by the **AAB (Ateliers d'Artistes de Belleville)** *(pick up studio maps at 32 rue de la Mare, 20th, www.ateliers-artistes-belleville.org)*. There are lots of funky bistros, cafés, and shops in the area.

A blast from the past, **Le Bistrot des Soupirs** (€-€€) *(49 rue de la Chine, 20th, 01-44.62.93.31)* hasn't changed since the 1950s; the bistro fare and wines are classic. Refined contemporary bistro cuisine, art-deco setting, and an animated ambience is what you get at **Le Zéphyr** (€€) *(1 rue Jourdain, 20th, 01-46.36.65.81)*. The wine bar **Le Baratin** (€-€€) *(3 rue Jouye-Rouve, 20th, 01-43.49.39.70)* serves generous portions of hearty food along with unusual wines. For great Thai, don't miss **Lao Siam** (€€) *(49 rue de Belleville, 19th, 01-40.40.09.68)*.

Alternative cool and streetwise urban chic reigns among young designers of **Rue Oberkampf**, where the bar scene buzzes at night. It all started with **Café Charbon** *(109 Rue Oberkampf, 11th, 01-43.57.55.13)*, the cool and stylish Belle-Époque music bar-café, and its nightclub annex **Nouveau Casino** *(01-43.57.57.40, www.nouveaucasino. net)*. Celebrities and locals love the trendy, arty bar **La Mère Lachaise** *(78 bd. de Ménilmontant, 20th, 01-47.97.61.60)*, with its fabulous terrace.

PARC DES BUTTES-CHAUMONT (6) *(19th)*

7 *to Louis Blanc, then*
7ᵇⁱˢ *to Buttes Chaumont or Botzaris*

Baron Haussmann converted a garbage dump and quarry on a hill into the **Parc des Buttes-Chaumont** *(Rue Manin, main entrance at Rue Armand Carrel, 01-53.35.89.35)*, located in a working-class neighborhood. A lake was created, with an island and footbridge, streams, a waterfall, and beaches. A Romanesque temple stands on the hilltop.

Inside the beautiful park **Pavillon Puebla** (€€€) *(01-42.08.92.62)* serves inventive French classics with a Catalan flavor. Artistry in Italian cuisine is what you get at the unpretentious but delicious **Chez Vincent** (€€) *(5 rue du Tunnel, 19th, 01-42.02.22.45)*. Incredible American chef

Mark Singer prepares fabulously imaginative new bistro fare at his restaurant **La Cave Gourmande (€€)** *(10 rue du Général-Brunet, 19th, 01-40.40.03.30).*

PARC DE LA VILLETTE: CITY OF SCIENCE; CITY OF MUSIC (7) (19th)

7 *to Porte de la Villette;* **5** *to Porte de Pantin*

Built on what was once the city's slaughterhouses and livestock market, the sprawling **Parc de la Villette** is home to an amazing complex of museums and exhibition halls. The **Cité des Sciences et de l'Industrie** *(30 ave. Corentin-Cariou, 19th, 01-40.05.80.00, www.cite-sciences.fr)* reveals the world of science and technology through multimedia exhibits, interactive displays, films, and conferences. The smaller **Cité de la Musique** *(221 ave. Jean-Jaurès, 19th, 01-44.84.44.84, www.cite-musique.fr)* houses, among other things, a music conservatory and a museum of music.

Head to **Avenue Jean-Jaurès** for meals or drinks. True to the district's old slaughterhouse renown, **Au Boeuf Couronné (€€€€)** *(188 ave. Jean-Jaurès, 19th, 01-42.39.44.44)* serves great classic beef dishes. In turn-of-the-century décor, **Dagorno (€€)** *(190 ave. Jean-Jaurès, 19th, 01-40.40.09.39)* serves wonderful traditional cuisine. **Café de la Musique (€€)** *(213 ave. Jean-Jaurès, 19th, 01-48.03.15.91)* is a trendy café better for people watching than meals.

FLEA MARKET OF ST-OUEN (8) *(18th)*

④ *to Porte de Clignancourt*

Extending across 15 acres, at the largest of Parisian flea markets, the **Marché aux Puces de St-Ouen** *(Main artery: Rue des Rosiers, St-Ouen, just north of the 18th, Sat.-Mon., 9 AM-6 PM)*, some 2,500 dealers sell antiques, artwork, furniture, books, jewelry, and odds and ends. The chic, cozy brasserie **Le Soleil (€€€)** *(109 ave. Michelet, St-Ouen, 01-40.10.08.08)* is a find in an area bereft of good restaurants.

LA GRANDE ARCHE DE LA DÉFENSE (9)
(NW border of Paris)

① *to La Défense/Grande Arche,*
Ⓐ *to La Défense/Grande Arche*

In 1981 President François Mitterand began a campaign to construct buildings with a cultural focus. Among the many creations that resulted from this project of "Grands Travaux," or "Great Works," some of the most spectacular are the Institute of the Arab World *(see Chapter 5, page 105)*, I.M. Pei's Louvre Pyramid *(see Chapter 2, page 45)*, the Opéra Bastille *(see Chapter 4, page 89)*, and the Grande Arche of La Défense.

La Défense is a large office building complex just beyond the northwestern edge of Paris. Built in the 1960s, its skyscrapers seemed to catapult French business into the supermodern era. Here, some of Europe's tallest buildings are the workplace of more than 100,000

SHORT EXCURSIONS OUTSIDE PARIS

Places to See:

1. Versailles
2. Chartres
3. Giverny
4. Fontainebleau
5. Malmaison
6. Chantilly
7. Reims
8. Disneyland Paris
9. Parc Astérix

When I go out into the countryside and see the sun and the green and everything flowering, I say to myself, "Yes indeed, all that belongs to me!"

—*Henri Rousseau*

These areas of historic significance, cultural interest, and natural beauty can each be seen in a day trip. All have hotels for those preferring overnight stays.

VERSAILLES (1)

RER: *C5 to Versailles Rive-Gauche/Château de Versailles*
Or SNCF Train: *Gare St-Lazare station to Versailles Rive-Droite; Gare Montparnasse station to Versailles-Chantiers (average travel time: 30-45 minutes)*

Louis XIV, the "Sun King," made the palace of **Versailles** *(01-30.83.76.20, info: 01-30.83.77.77, www. chateauversailles.fr)* into the symbol of absolute monarchy. It remained the seat of royal political power from 1682 until the Revolution, a century later. The resplendent château, the largest in Europe, lodged 20,000 people at a time. Ornate and luxurious, it is surrounded by formal gardens with statues, canals, pools, and fountains. Louis XIV held extravagant parties and receptions here. He built a smaller palace, the **Grand Trianon**, for himself and his mistress. Later, Louis XV built the **Petit Trianon**, his own retreat, which became Marie-Antoinette's favorite.

A good seafood restaurant is **Marée de Versailles** (€€) *(22 rue au Pain, Versailles, 01-30.21.73.73)*. Tiny, quaint **Le Potager du Roy** (€€€) *(1 rue du Maréchal-Joffre, Versailles,*

01-39.50.35.34) serves traditional French food. Exquisite haute cuisine in an elegant ambience is a near-regal experience at **Les Trois Marches (€€€)** *(Hôtel Trianon Palace, 1 bd. de la Reine, Versailles, 01-39.50. 13.21)*. For more info, restaurants, and accommodations, contact the **Versailles Tourist Office** *(Sofitel Building, 2 bis, ave. de Paris, 01-39.24.88.88, www. versailles-tourisme.com)*.

CHARTRES (2)

SNCF Train: *Gare Montparnasse station to Chartres (average travel time: 1 hour)*

The magnificent Gothic cathedral of **Chartres** *(02-37.21.75.02, www.chartres.com)* is noted for its incredible stained-glass windows and its elaborately sculpted statues and reliefs. Behind the cathedral, the **Musée des Beaux-Arts** *(02-37.36.41.39)* holds Renaissance paintings and tapestries. The **Maison de l'Archéologie** *(14 rue St-Pierre, 02-37.30.99.38)* recounts the story of the excavation of a Gallo-Roman city. A path along the banks of the Eure River leads to the ruins of the old Roman city wall.

There are plenty of restaurants in town; **L'Estocade (€-€€)** *(1 rue de la Porte-Guillaume, 02-37.34.27.17)* has a river view. For accommodations and other info, go to the **Chartres Tourist Office** *(pl. Cathédrale, 02-37.18.26.26)*.

GIVERNY (3)

SNCF Train: *Gare St-Lazare station to Vernon, then 3-mile taxi ride or bus (average travel time: 1 hour)*

Claude Monet lived in **Giverny** with his mistress and eight children and created his superb Impressionist paintings there. The famous water-lily pond, with its weeping willows and Japanese bridge, is a favorite spot. The house-museum, **Fondation Claude Monet** *(84 rue de Claude Monet, 02-32.51.28.21, www.fondation-monet. com; get there early)*, has no original Monets but plenty of memorabilia. Nearby, the **Musée Américain de Giverny** *(99 rue Claude Monet, 02-32.51.94.65, www.maag.org)* is dedicated to American Impressionists who worked in France in Monet's time.

The famous **Hôtel Baudy (€)** *(81 rue Claude-Monet, 02-32.21.10.03, reserve ahead)* is a museum-restaurant where some of Monet's American followers lived and worked. For overnight stays, **La Musardiere (€)** *(Rue Claude Monet, 02-32.21.03.18)* is a lovely hotel dating back to 1880. It also features a restaurant with a terrace and garden. **Le Coin des Artistes (€)** *(65 rue Claude-Monet, 02-32.21.36.77)* is a B&B with an art gallery. For more info on Giverny, restaurants, and lodgings, go to *http://giverny.org*.

SNCF Train: *Gare de Lyon station to Fontainebleau-Avon, then bus AB, marked "Château" (buy a "Forfait Château de Fontainebleau" ticket, which includes train and bus fare, château entrance fee, and audio guide) (average travel time: 1 hour)*

Though not as sprawling or magnificent as Versailles, the **Château de Fontainebleau** *(01-60.71.50.70, www.musee-chateau-fontainebleau.fr)*, residence of French rulers, underwent transformations that give it a mix of styles. Napoleon I built an ornate throne room and his own extravagant quarters in the palace. Explore the wonderful gardens and forest.

Rue Grande is dotted with restaurants. Try the creative cuisine at **Au Délice Impérial** (€-€€) *(1 rue Grande, 01-64.22.20.70)*. Heavy oak tables and tapestries give classic meals at **Le Caveau des Ducs** (€-€€) *(24 rue de Ferrare, 01-64.22.05.05)* a 17th-century country flavor. **Aigle Noir Hôtel** (€€) *(27 pl. Napoléon-Bonaparte, 01-60.74.60.00, www.hotelaiglenoir.fr)*, built in the 15th century, sits across from the Fontainebleau castle gardens. You'll feel at home in its warm, elegant rooms. Elegant **Hôtel Napoléon** (€€) *(9 rue Grande, 01-60.39.50.50, www.hotelnapoleon-fontainebleau.com)* is footsteps away from the château and provides a refined and charming setting. For info and maps, as well as bike rentals, go to the **Fontainebleau Area Tourist Office** *(4 rue Royale, 01-60.74.99.99, www. fontainebleau-tourisme.com)*.

MALMAISON (5)

RER: *A1 to La Défense, then bus 258 (travel time varies depending on your starting point in Paris)*

Napoleon and Josephine's love-nest **Malmaison** (*Ave. du Château, 92500 Rueil-Malmaison, 01-41.29.05.55, www.chateau-malmaison.fr, www.napoleon.org*) became her home after the divorce. The museum is dedicated to Napoleon and the First Empire. Don't miss Josephine's famous rose garden.

CHANTILLY (6)

SNCF Train: *Gare du Nord station to Chantilly-Gouvieux (average travel time: 30 minutes on train, plus 5-minute walk to town, 20-minute walk to château)*

Chantilly, domain of the Condé Princes, is known for its lace, for the invention of Chantilly whipped cream and for its equestrian history of prestigious horseraces and hunting forests. The fairy tale **castle of Chantilly**, with its parks and incredible stables, houses the **Condé Museum** (*03-44.62.62.62, www.cheateauchantilly.com*), with

works by Raphael, Botticelli, Giotto, and Holbein. The **Musée Vivant du Cheval** (*Les Grandes Écuries, 03-44.57.40.40, www.museevivantducheval.fr*), in the Grandes Écuries stables, shows horses and gives riding displays (first Sunday of every month).

Every June, high society descends on the Chantilly race-course for the flat-racing trophies, a prestigious and fashionable event.

The tea room in the hamlet of the castle, **Aux Goûters Champêtres (€)** *(03-44.57.46.21)*, features the famous whipped cream. On Chantilly's main street, the cozy bistro **Le Goutillon (€)** *(61 rue du Connétable, 03-44. 58.01.00)* offers home-style cooking. For info, restaurants, and lodgings, contact the **Chantilly Tourist Office** *(60 ave. Maréchal-Joffre, 03-44.67.37.37, www.chantilly-tourisme.com)*, near the station.

REIMS (7)

SNCF Train: *Gare de l'Est station to Reims*
(average travel time: 90 minutes)

Most French monarchs were crowned in Reims. **Notre-Dame de Reims** *(1 rue Guillaume de Machault, 03-26.47.55.34, www.cathedrale-reims.com)* is an ornately decorated Gothic cathedral with many beautiful stained-glass windows, including some of Chagall's designs. Located in the region of Champagne, the area is home to France's finest bubbly. Visits to champagne houses are by appointment only: **Pommery** *(5 pl. du Général Gouraud, 03-26.61.62.63, www.pommery.com)*, **Krug** *(5 rue Coquebert, 03-26.84.44.20)*, **Veuve Clicquot** *(1 pl. des Droits-de-l'Homme, 03-26.89.54.41)*, **Lanson** *(12 bd. Lundy, 03-26.78.50.50)*, and **Roederer** *(21 bd. Lundy, 03-26.40.42.11, by appointment and recommendation)*. At **Épernay** (18 miles away), **Moët et Chandon**

(20 ave. de Champagne, Épernay, 03-26.51.20.00, www.moet.com) and **Mercier** *(68 ave. de Champagne, Épernay, 03-26.51.22.22, www.champagne-mercier.fr)* do great tours.

You can find many cafés and brasseries on **Place Drouet d'Erlon** that serve good meals. Try **Aux Coteaux (€)** *(86-88 pl. Drouet d'Erlon, 03-26.47.38.84)* for tasty pizza and other delicious dishes. For overnight stays, **Ariston Fils Champagne (€)** *(4-8 Grande Rue, Brouillet, 03-26.97. 43.46)* offers rooms in working champagne vineyards. For more info, contact the **Reims Tourist Office** *(2 rue Guillaume de Machault, 03-26.77.45.00, www.reims-tourisme.com)*. In the town of **Épernay**, **La Cave à Champagne (€)** *(16 rue Gambetta, Épernay, 03-26.55. 50.70)* is a good classic bistro. And if you get full from your meal, and fancy an overnight stay, the **Hôtel de Champagne (€)** *(30 rue Eugène-Mercier, Épernay, 03-26. 53.10.60)* is a comfortable hotel chain.

THEME PARKS: MICKEY AND ASTÉRIX

DISNEYLAND PARIS (8)
RER: *A4 to Marne-la-Vallée/Chessy.*
(One-day RER + Disneyland Paris tickets
sold at major metro stations.)

Disneyland Paris *(Marne-la-Vallée, 01-60.30.60.30,*
www.disneylandparis.com) has all the usual Disney fun.

PARC ASTÉRIX (9)
RER: *B3 to Roissy/Aéroport Charles-de-Gaulle 1,*
then shuttle bus (platform A3)

At **Parc Astérix** *(60128 Plailly, 08-26.30.10.40, www.*
parcasterix.fr) the Gauls compete with Disney.

INDEX